Stock Trading for Beginners

Unbreakable Strategies on How to Invest in Stocks, Options, Forex and Futures. Generate Cash Flow and Create Financial Freedom with Swing and Day Trading for a Living

By Paul Cohen

Table of Contents

Introduction

If you are thinking about financially securing your future, then you are probably considering whether to start a savings plan or to invest your money. While a savings plan is appealingly risk-free, investing guarantees you so much more in terms of returns. Because banks give a fixed rate of return on money saved with them, you can be sure about the money you should expect at the end of your savings period by using simply saving calculators.

With stocks, the rate of return is so much higher than savings, but then so is the risk. As the interest rates of banks fluctuate with the economy, the stock market fluctuates on the principles of supply and demand. Sometimes the stock market performs very well (bull market), and sometimes growth is sluggish (bear market). In adverse situations, like the 2008 stock market crash, stock investments can be wiped out completely. The high returns and accompanying high risk of the stock market compare rather garishly against the low returns and low risk of savings as far as a savings plan for your future goes.

Stock investing is a rather straightforward endeavor that nonetheless requires that you develop a certain set of skills and build your knowledge on the entire workings of the financial institutions. Understanding is crucial to the mastery of a subject. It converts you from a bumbling amateur to, well, not exactly a Warren Buffett–type investor but one that is sufficiently informed so that they don't make mistakes that could turn out to be calamitous to their savings. Information is the most important tool for investing in the stock market. It comes in handy in understanding stock market operations as well as when you get down to the real transacting (there's enough time to get to that later).

This book is meant to improve your knowledge of the operations of the stock market, enabling you to understand ways of making good money in investing even while holding on to your main job. I believe that the topics discussed here will arm you with enough information to turn you into a fairly able investor, one that makes distinctly more money in interest on their investment than the bank could possibly give. By following this book's practical and simply written guide on stock market investing, it is our hope that you will become a better investor and convert your current savings into so much more.

Chapter 1: Introduction to the Stock Market

To understand the history of the stock market, we should have a grasp of the inner workings of a stock exchange first—specifically the bid-ask spread that also influences the prices of shares. The bid-ask spread is a sort of register that consolidates the demand and supply of a stock in a central position. On the one hand, it allows people who need to buy stocks to place an order of the number and price of shares they intend to buy. On the other, it gives the sellers an opportunity to list the number of shares they intend to sell, as well as the target price for them. The final price of the stock depends on whether the buyer is willing to settle for the price of the buyer or whether the buyer is able to buy the stocks at their listed price. The laws of demand and supply also come into play, with buyers being forced to increase their purchase price when the competition is higher and sellers accepting a lower price for their stocks if there are not enough buyers to drive demand and price up.

Now, the stock exchange facilitates this conversion of ownership from the seller to the buyer by bringing them together in one platform. It is essentially a platform comprising of stockbrokers where they congregate to perform the business of exchanging (buying and selling) stocks. But who exactly runs the stock exchange? The stock exchanges as they currently exist were founded so long ago that the issue of who owns them seems immaterial. For the most part, the stock exchange is just the building or platform on which brokers buy and sell. The most important aspect of the stock exchange is the stocks that are listed in it. And because companies only list where they can be sure of attracting investors (stockholders), this is a very important aspect of their operations. It is no surprise, therefore, that the oldest bourses were started as corporations by stockbrokers to facilitate the exchange of securities among themselves.

The stock market has had a long and eventful history, one that is almost as long as the banking industry, by far the oldest financial institution still surviving today.

1100S–1400S

The earliest versions of the stock market were rather different from the bourse as we know it today. In France, the country of origin for these early stock exchanges, *courtiers de change* agents oversaw the agricultural debts issued by banks to farmers all over the state. They could swap and renegotiate these debts, an equity exchange that formed the foundation for the current stock market. Over time, the business of exchanging debts grew, and these men expanded to new markets, including government securities. As the first stockbrokers, the Venetian *courtiers de change* established stocks as a legitimate way for "common" people to make money in the financial markets.

Interestingly, these men carried on a system of cross-transactions with each other, buying debt and equity of each other based on risk and various other factors. Because they represented different banks in the debt issuance and collection sector, this interlinkage would later evolve to become the present-day interbank lending system, whereby banks issue each other with cheaper short-term loans. The people involved in this trade were mostly commodity traders, with the value of commodities changing hands but not the commodities themselves. This was a virtualization of the business functions that was way ahead of its time at the time.

The merchants of Venice started trading in government securities in the early thirteenth century. They were soon followed by banks in Verona, Genoa, Florence, and Pisa as it became evident that government securities presented a wonderful investment opportunity. Trading between the merchants was done by word of mouth and handwritten agreements. The extent of organized trading was limited to the houses of prominent traders where many of these *courtiers de change* could congregate and negotiate terms and conduct their transactions.

From France, the development of the securities market moved to Belgium and Netherlands, where traders started stock markets in Antwerp, Bruges, Ghent, and Rotterdam between the 1400s and the 1500s. In Antwerp, a clan of traders named the Van der Beurze family established a hub for stock traders to exchange equities, forming the first formalized stock market, except it still traded in agricultural debts, commodities, and government bonds. The concept of private companies using the stock markets to raise money had not yet been born.

1500s–1700s

In the meantime, before the first publicly traded company made it into the bourse, England joined in the "stock" trading enterprise. As usual, government securities were the main commodities traded, but debts and commodities also changed hands. By this time, as European civilizations continued to expand, there was a stock market in pretty much every country that had a banking industry. Business ownership also started to change, with partnerships and corporations becoming increasingly popular as businessmen recognized the profit of combining their financial muscle. New philosophies of a business organization birthed the limited liability system of business organization and paved the way for the modern conglomerate.

The first publicly traded company would emerge from an unexpected area: risk. Explorers had discovered the West Indies as a land filled with business opportunities and tremendous riches, but the sea routes they took exposed them to piracy, with numerous voyages turning up zero returns because a ship was ransacked at sea. In fact, losing a ship meant that the trader who had put up the money for the voyage, including the commodities to be bartered for gold and other treasure, wound up losing a ton of money.

To reduce the risk of losing a merchant ship at sea, a group of traders formed the East India Company, with each owning a portion of the assets but shielded from personal liability for any losses suffered beyond their investment in that particular expedition. This format of overseas trading quickly caught on. By keeping one's eggs in separate baskets, so to say, traders could have one out of three or four of their invested ships lost at sea and still end up making some money from the transaction.

As shareholding in a company became more and more liberalized, the Dutch East India Company became, in 1602, the first publicly traded company. Every share was entitled to an equal percentage of the proceeds of the company's profits. However, the trading of shares was not done in dedicated exchange houses. For example, the business of the New York Stock Exchange was conducted in coffee shops. Brokers would meet in coffee shops and conduct their business there, but this soon proved to be too ineffective, and the business of trading shares was moved into the stock exchanges.

The systems that even today moderate stock trading were put in place back then, enabling the traders to physically identify the person with the shares they wanted, approach them, and negotiate to buy them off. The counter was soon discovered to be a better alternative to tracking down traders with a particular stock. People intending to sell would just list their shares at the counter, and people wanting to buy would place their orders at the counter. An easy and effective system of centralized control was established, but having a centralized buy/sell counter meant that the market forces of demand and supply were also let loose. Someone with a stock could wait until so many orders had been placed that they could name their price, however exorbitant, and get a buyer. The book value of the stock, which had been the only moderating factor before trading floors and counters were opened up, was no longer the sole determinant of the value at which the stock would sell anymore.

Even though the Amsterdam Stock Exchange was the first to have a publicly listed company, the London Stock Exchange quickly gained prominence as the foremost bourse in Europe, bolstered by the spirited expansion of the British Empire. When the stock markets started, they were simply a congregation of businessmen who sought to establish a better working environment for their activities dealing in agricultural debt and other commodities. The progression to trading in the shares of companies happened over a few hundred years. But even with this growth, the full potential of the stock market was not realized by the government or the investors themselves. While the usefulness of stockholding to reduce risk and make business more profitable was recognized, the effect that this particular institution would have on the rest of the business institutions escaped the attention of everyone involved.

1700s–1800s

The ease with which a business could raise the money to invest in infrastructure and expand its operations acted as a stimulus to other sectors of the economy. A few centuries before, the industrial revolution had transformed the whole business environment of the European continent, transforming it from an agrarian economy into an industry-based one. Even as these changes swept through the continent, the equities industry pretty much grew unregulated, with businesses being formed overnight, issuing shares with little supervision from the government and very little accountability to shareholders.

The bubble soon burst, and many listed companies could no longer afford to pay dividends to their shareholders. As the regulatory body responsible for the biggest stock exchange in the continent at the time, the government of England stepped in to mitigate the situation with a ban on listings in the London Stock Exchange that extended all the way to the year 1825. The delay allowed the New York Stock Exchange, which started in 1817, to flourish. New companies that could not go public in London opted for the American bourse. Furthermore, the NYSE was located at the epicenter of US trade and commerce, and even though it was not the first stock exchange established in the new world, it consolidated itself into the biggest and most competitive stock exchange the world over.

Modern Stock Markets

Even though governments have never been directly involved in the operations of the stock markets, regulations were enacted all through the nineteenth and twentieth centuries to formalize the operations of bourses even as their importance to the economy rose to greater heights. The need for corporations to raise money for expansion made it necessary for stock exchanges to be established in nearly every country by the middle twentieth century. Today, as much as one trillion worth of stocks are traded in stock exchanges around the world.

As the number of people interested in investing in the stock market increased, media attention and the need for information necessitated the formation of industry measures of stock market performance, taking into consideration the trends observed in the strongest companies in a stock exchange to estimate the overall performance of the bourse. These measures are called indexes. They include the Dow Jones, Standard & Poor, and the NASDAQ-100 among others. Specialized indexes have been formulated to measure the performance of various sectors of the economy by the performance of the stocks of companies that dominate them.

The current stock market is highly globalized. Investors in America can easily invest in Chinese companies listed in China or America and vice versa, simply because stockbrokers are allowed to trade in pretty much any stock market around the world. From international to regional indexes, progress has been directed heavily toward the global stock market as a whole. Mergers between stock exchanges have been increasing gradually since the turn of the century. The fact that stock exchanges are independent entities that are largely unregulated by state bodies in the scope of their operations allows for mergers and partnerships that have pushed the boundaries, pushing gradually toward a unified world stock market.

Stock Exchanges

As the world stock market developed, various exchanges evolved to appeal to certain industries based on the kind of stockbrokers that transact in them. A certain pattern of specialization has emerged in some of the biggest bourses, with some countries proving to be conducive to companies in certain sectors of the economy. For example, the Canadian Stock Exchange, commonly known as the TSX, has a higher number of companies in the oil and gas sector than every other bourse. Because it allows companies based in the country as well as the rest of the world to be listed and because the country, with a huge portion of the Arctic region open to it, is a leader in the oil and gas industry, these types of companies have gravitated toward a listing there.

Understanding the specialization of a stock exchange can really help you as an investor to know what exchanges to target in your hunt for stocks. With the stock market virtually blown open by digital technology infrastructure, you need not confine yourself to one stock exchange, even if it is the NYSE, the world's largest by market capitalization, or the NASDAQ, which ranks second.

The New York Stock Exchange

The NYSE is the leading stock exchange, not only in America but also in the world. It has the biggest market capitalization of any other stock exchange in the world. So big, in fact, that the combined value of companies listed in the NYSE is greater than the combined capitalization of the next three biggest stock exchanges. As part of its efforts to continue dominating the world stock market, the NYSE in 2007 merged with the Euronext to create the first truly transatlantic stock exchange.

Established in 1792 with the signing of the Buttonwood Agreement by a group of 24 stockbrokers, the bourse has grown to incorporate over 1,000 stockbrokers on the trading floor and tens of other brokers who are affiliated with partner firms. The NYSE was started at the tail end of the old stock trading world order where trading in securities was done by a loosely affiliated network of brokers in the various regions of the world. After 25 years of operating from coffee shops, the stockbrokers reorganized, instituted reforms on fair play and stock manipulation, and adopted electrical telegraph technology to increase the effectiveness of trading in 1817. They also established a dedicated building where all their transactions would be carried out—the first stock trading establishment in America. By merging with other organizations of brokers, the NYSE gradually established its dominance in the world stock market by increasing membership and trade volumes, soon overtaking the Philadelphia Stock Exchange, the oldest stock exchange in the United States by age of establishment.

The London Stock Exchange

The London Stock Exchange is the biggest stock market in England and Europe. Some of the largest companies in the continent are listed in the course, as well as some giants in the world stage. Even though the NYSE enjoys the distinction of being the biggest bourse in the world, the LSE is decidedly the most international of all stock markets, with companies from over 60 countries in all parts of the world listed. The LSE is also linked with the Italian stock exchange to form the London Stock Exchange Group.

Even though the LSE was founded in 1698, it wasn't until 1801 that it was formally registered as part of the effort by the government of England to bring the then extremely wayward stock market under control. For over 25 years of its existence until 1825, the LSE was barred from listing new companies, a fact that allowed the NYSE, considerably younger and located out of Europe (then the world epicenter of finance and business) to gain an advantage and grow unchecked.

NASDAQ

In the 1970s, the dominance of the NYSE, the world's largest stock market by capitalization, was challenged by the newly formed NASDAQ stock exchange. This innovative new bourse was formed by a partnership between the National Association of Securities Dealers and the Financial Industry Regulatory Authority. It eliminated entirely the need for a physical location for a stock exchange, a building where brokers meet and exchange stocks among themselves. By using a network of computers, the NASDAQ was able to reduce the bid-ask spread and increase the effectiveness of the process substantially. Soon, the rest of the industry followed the path blazed by the NASDAQ, going electronic to increase efficiency. However, most stock exchanges have maintained the physical location of their activities, hybridizing their operations between electronic and on-the-floor trading.

Since its establishment, NASDAQ has grown in leaps and bounds and is currently the second-biggest stock exchange in the world. The bourse started off as a quotation system that combined technology with stock trading to facilitate electronic transactions through the traditional on-the-floor transactions, but it gradually built its trading capabilities, eventually becoming the biggest virtual stock exchange in the world. Nasdaq Inc., the parent company of NASDAQ, has proven to be quite enterprising, actively seeking mergers, partnerships, and buyouts of other stock exchanges to consolidate its operations globally. Some of its most ambitious consolidation efforts include the OMX merger in 2010 that allowed it to operate in the Nordic countries and the ultimately unsuccessful bid for the NYSE.

The Tokyo Stock Exchange

The Tokyo Stock Exchange is the largest bourse in Asia and the fourth biggest in the world based on the market cap of the companies listed. Unlike the other large stock exchanges in the world, the TSE was established with the help of the government in 1878. Up until 1942, the Tokyo Stock Exchange was just one of ten bourses that facilitated stock trading in cities across the country. In the year 1943, all the stock markets were combined into the TSE. Even though the TSE has faced some problems with its systems, it still holds a strategic position as the gateway to the Asia region and has been forming partnerships with other bourses like the LSE in the face of a highly competitive international stock market.

Euronext

In 2000, the Brussels Stock Exchange, the Paris Bourse, and the Amsterdam Stock Exchange merged to form Euronext. The merger was made possible by the synchronization of financial systems in Eurozone countries. At a €3.8 trillion valuation, the Euronext replaces the LSE as the biggest bourse in Europe and also claims its position as the fourth largest in the world.

Stock Market Crashes in History
The Wall Street Crash of 1929

Even as large-scale farming practices drove down prices and wreaked havoc in the agricultural sector, the view among the American public was that the stock market bull run that has started soon after the war would continue forever. Another cause for the bull run was widespread speculation in the stock markets.

The initial problem came about in March 1929 with a warning by the Federal Reserve on the dangers of continued speculation in the stock market. Investors started pulling their money off the stock market, but assurances by the National City Bank that people could access cheap credit offered a short respite. Even though the whole economy was sluggish with declining sales of cars, high consumer debt, a sluggish construction industry, and declining production of steel in the mills scattered around the country, the bull run continued undeterred. In fact, the Dow Jones rose over 20% between June and September to peak at 380.

From this high point, the stock market started a slow decline that many people dismissed as a healthy correction. Some pundits went as far as advising people to buy because the market would pick right up and continue with its stratospheric rise. However, events overseas created some very deep concerns. In London, a prominent British investor named Clarence Hatry was sent to prison after being found guilty of forgery with the intention to defraud. This arrest precipitated a phenomenal crash in the London stock market, which in turn jarred the confidence of American investors.

Another attempt by bankers to placate the public created another temporary respite, but this one lasted just two days. By Monday morning, the panic selling started again in real earnest. The Dow fell 13% by the end of the day and then lost another 12% points on Tuesday. By November, the Dow was down to 198 points from a high of 381 just two months before. In the end, the crash had wiped as much as $40 billion from the US economy. The country would need almost the whole of the 1930–1940 decade recovering the massive losses suffered.

The Stock Market Crash of 1973–1974

On January 9, 1973, *Time Magazine* predicted that 1973 would be a gilt-edged year that portended huge gains in the stock market and the economy as a whole. Just two days later, the Dow Jones started the plummet that would culminate with it down 45%. This time, the public had little to do with the decline. In the months preceding the extended crash, the US dollar had been devalued, the country was in shock over the Watergate scandal, Bretton Wood systems had slowly collapsed after struggling with bad debt, and the economy was experiencing a recession. At least, in this case, the stock market did not stand a chance. The odds stacked against it were too high.

With it, the stock market brought down GDP growth from 7.2% to −2.1% and sent the economy into a spiral of inflation that peaked at 12.3% in 1974. And just like the 1929 Wall Street Crash, the United Kingdom stock market was brought down, too, losing 73% at the same time the American market was hemorrhaging. The UK economy, too, was not spared. GDP growth faltered from a high of 5.1% to −1.1%. The property market also suffered greatly, with the Bank of England being forced to bail out some of the country's lenders. Inflation in Britain continued to rise past the crash to peak at 25% in the year 1975.

Black Monday

As economic globalization swept around the world, stock markets became increasingly interlinked. And with the recent advent of technology use in stock exchanges, brokerage firms were increasingly using automated selling and buying techniques. Because of this, the response to a sustained attack on American warships in the high seas by Iranian silkworm missiles (potential trigger for war) spread alarm across the world. In the closing hours of the Hong Kong Stock Exchange, widespread panic selling caused the exchange to decline in a very short time and start a chain reaction of massive declines in London, Madrid, Australian, and American stock exchanges.

The Black Monday crash holds the record for the largest decline in the Dow average in a single day (23%). But interestingly enough, even this decline was totally uncalled for. As stated above, the greatest cause for the decline was the fact that automatic sell/buy price triggers were widely in use by investors, which meant that the calming human element of crisis transactions was not in play during this period. After this crash, regulations were put in place to prevent similar panic selling in the form of circuit breakers or trading curbs.

With circuit breakers, trading is halted the moment indices register mass sell orders that could potentially cause massive drops in prices of the whole stock market. Depending on the percentage drop in the index, trading can be closed for one hour to one day. Circuit breakers mitigate against market crashes and reduce the damage in the event that a crash is inevitable.

The Dot-Com Bubble

Also known as the internet bubble, this crash, starting in the millennial year 2000, occurred after almost a decade of oversubscription to the IPOs of tech companies and an accompanying rise in demand for their issued shares that drove prices through the roof. Just like with any bubble, emotions trounced logic as investors overlooked metrics like price-earnings ratio and other technical ratios to continue buying shares of internet companies even when they were overpriced a few times over their real value.

The public joined in the fray of stock trading, with people quitting their jobs to focus their energies on stock trading, fueled by feverish media attention to the huge profits people were making in internet stocks. So wild was the bubble that internet companies could go public with no revenues or real profits. The founders and employees of these dot-com start-ups became instant millionaires. So, what if they could not yet access their money because it was locked up by the regulatory SEC restrictions? The prices just kept climbing and climbing— all the more money they would make when they could finally start selling.

In the end, confidence would turn out to be the trigger that caused the bubble to burst. All through the bubble period culminating in December 1999, the interest rates were considerably low as the government anticipated a phenomenon described by pundits as the Year 2000 problem. However, when no such thing manifested, the Fed announced plans to increase interest rates in February 2000, starting fears of greater volatility in the stock market. However, the bubble continued undaunted, and the NASDAQ-100 Index reached 5,050.

But after a series of downturns, including a failed merger between Yahoo! and eBay, the bankruptcy of Pets.com, and a series of accounting scandals between 2001 and 2002, the stock market corrected and sent the NASDAQ-100 plummeting 78% in October 2002. The dot-com bubble had come and gone and the economy was left smarting from the loss of $5 trillion in total market capitalization. However, the biggest legacy of the dot-com bubble was that it created a glut of office furniture and equipment as offices closed up. Many programmers were also forced to go back to university and acquire the law and accounting degrees they had forfeited to take programming courses and jump into the dot-com bandwagon.

The Stock Market Crash of 2008

The stock market crash of 2008 was the culmination of a decade of misdeeds in the US financial market. Interest rates were maintained at 1% by the Fed starting in 2003, ostensibly to allow the market to recover from the dot-com bubble burst. The low-interest rates encouraged massive borrowing, which the real estate market took as an opportunity to encourage massive home purchases. Mortgages were offered at subprime rates, encouraging even more massive borrowing. For the financial markets, a glaring lack of insight caused giants like AIG and Lehman Brothers to overinvest in repackaged subprime loans.

When the real estate bubble burst and borrowers were unable to pay, foreclosures and defaulted payments affected not just the lenders but also the investment banks that had provided them with an endless supply of cash to loan out. AIG was soon in deep trouble, and so were Lehman Brothers and tens of other banks and investment institutions.

In the end, the whole sorry situation sent the whole banking industry into a tailspin of failed giants and massive foreclosures. After more than two years of escalation and tensions in the stock market, Lehman Brothers was forced to file for bankruptcy. As one of the oldest traded companies and a perceived sure bet, the companies that no one ever expects to fail, the folding up of Lehman Brothers caused investors to rush the turnstiles as they sought to divest themselves of their stock holdings. Between September 2008 and March 2009, the stock market lost 50% of its value as indicated by the Dow Jones Index.

Chapter 2: Get Started with Stocks

Stocks represent a unit of ownership that is issued by companies to the general public, allowing them to take possession of its assets and earnings. It is this claim to earnings that justifies earnings distribution to shareholders in the form of dividends. By simple calculation, an investor's claim to the assets of a company in which they hold shares increases as the percentage of their share ownership increases.

First off, a stake in a company does not really equate to a stake in its assets. Your shares do not really make you a partial owner of the corporation you hold shares in because shares are issued by companies as more of a stake in their financial performance than the conventional kind of ownership. Corporations, being legally recognized persons, own their assets, file their own taxes, are sued, and sue other legal entities, and have the ability to take loans for their own expedient use.

So, does owning the stocks of a company equate with the right to their assets? Not by a long shot. The principle of separation of rights and control governs the way shareholders interact with the assets of holding companies. With this principle, your share ownership is restricted to the amount of equity a company has offered to the public, not their assets, or even a portion of the company equivalent to the percentage of shares you own. This separation of shareholders' equity and the corporation itself is very important because it restricts liability for both. Even in the event of a bankruptcy, only the company's held assets may be sold. Your stake will remain as a nominal value of whatever value the stock market places on the company. In those adverse events, only the value of your shares will drop, but your ownership of them is not enforceable by any state body, which is to say that not even the courts can compel you to sell—you decide. For the corporation, its assets are protected from appropriation even by the shareholders who purportedly own a share of the business.

Even though shares do not constitute ownership rights in a business, they do equate to voting rights during shareholder meetings. The shareholder is also entitled to a share of the company's profits in dividends for those companies that reward its shareholders with them. Higher up in the share ownership hierarchy, shareholders also have enough voting power to be involved in seating the board of directors. In large corporations, the board of directors runs the company on behalf of the shareholders by appointing the senior managers, crafting the long-term strategy of the business, and authorizing massive expenditures like acquisitions.

If stocks are not really a portion of the company a shareholder buys, then what exactly are they? In many instances, companies issue stocks to the public to raise large amounts of money, distributing the capital risk to thousands (or millions) of people. Money raised in the initial public offering is then used to fund new business projects and propel it to greater heights. Some companies, like software giant Microsoft, went public because of government regulations that require companies with a certain number of shareholders (over 500) to release their financial reports publicly. Rather than release financial reports like publicly traded companies but not enjoy the surplus of capital that comes with a public issue, companies like these opt to issue a portion of the business to the public. Another motivation for issuing the shares of a company to the public is to make it possible for employees to trade out their stakes in a company (usually offered as an incentive during employment) for real cash.

The stock market is the institution through which brokers and traders exchange their shares with other traders and brokers. A large number of them are involved in the stock trade whose liquidity of shares is quite high—there is always a willing buyer and a willing seller. Stock markets also facilitate the transfer of bonds and other securities. Only in the stock market can a shareholder hope to turn their stocks into liquid cash, especially because, as mentioned above, the assets of the company whose shares they hold are out of bounds.

There are two types of stocks issued by corporations—common and preferred.

Comparison

What we have discussed above is essentially the common stock type of share ownership. Common stocks enable a person to hold a portion of a business but not take possession of it even though it gives them a limited right to influence the business operations of a company. On the other hand, preferred stocks, a hybrid share that is issued by a company for a very specific capital requirement, gives the holder zero say on a business's running—no voting rights, no right to influence the board of directors' placement, and no consultation in the making of huge business decisions. For that reason, preferred stocks are a little more like bonds than shares.

Investors with common stocks are entitled to a share of the company's profits in the form of dividends. These dividends are determined by the board of directors on a per-share basis. As for preferred stockholders, their claim to dividends is usually greater, taking precedence over common shareholders in terms of yield per share and priority. In the event of a company missing a dividend payout, preferred shareholders receive their arrears first. Preferred stockholder also takes precedence over common stockholders in the event of a company liquidating its operations. In fact, because of the greater claim of common stockholders to the business as owners (making decisions, voting, etc.), they are paid absolutely last behind holders of bonds, credit, and preferred shares.

The common stock is the most popular type of share for people to transact in. It performs much better than preferred shares in the stock market, but it is also more volatile. With a flexible interest rate, the return on capital invested in stock is determined solely by the perception of the stock market on the company's financial strength. The fixed interest rate of the preferred stock makes it less susceptible to market volatility in the stock market. Instead, their value is affected by interest rates of the general economy in an inverse manner. When the interest rates rise, the value of a preferred stock drops, and when it declines, their value climbs.

Another important distinction between common shares and preferred ones is the rights of the issuer to call them back. While common stocks may only be bought back in the event of a company going bankrupt or folding, preferred stocks may be repurchased at a prefixed time or any time the company decides to call them back. The company then pays shareholders a redemption rate to investors, often a higher rate of return than expected. One of the factors that influence the price of preferred stocks is actually the anticipation of a callback. The sooner a company is likely to call back preferred shares issued to the public, the more in demand those shares become as investors seek to capitalize on the premium redemption rate.

Bonds

Bonds have been in existence since time immemorial. They were used by ancient governments to raise money for various capital-intensive causes, which is the same use to which they are put even today. So, what exactly are bonds? In the stock trading sense of the word, a bond is like a unit of a bigger loan that a company or government takes from a large pool of investors for a specific purpose. The whole loan, thus taken, also falls under the definition of a bond. What individual investors hold in their hands as the bond is usually the certificate given to signify the borrower/lender relationship they enter into with the borrower. In the bond certificate, the terms of payment and details of the loan are indicated, including the interest rate and maturity date. Trading in bonds can either be over the counter in the bourse or between lender and borrower.

How Bonds Work

The system of bond borrowing can be traced way back to the ancient Mesopotamian financial systems, where corporations borrowed grain with the promise to pay back the principal plus interest at a certain date. Instead of placing the company assets as surety, a bond was used instead, symbolizing the borrower's deepest commitment to repay the loan. This obligation to repay the debt became to represent the bond the current world knows as financial systems evolved. Bonds are necessitated by a number of realities that only the insider might know about the capital markets.

The capital requirements of large corporations are quite extensive. To start a new project, finance ongoing operations (especially in R & D), and repay old debts that have not been repaid yet, companies need to raise massive amounts of money. From large infrastructural projects to war efforts, governments have an appetite for capital that is tax remissions from citizens and businesses do not meet.

In some cases, the banks cannot meet the demand for these needs simply because the amount of money these entities require is so great. The risk of a bank going under in the event of these massive borrowers defaulting is too great, which means that corporations and governments have to become creative about how they raise the money for whatever their super-important need might be.

The way to do this is by distributing the risk to so many people that the effect of a possible default is blunted by the very fact that it is spread over many people. Having 10,000 people risk $1,000 each is preferable to one entity risking the $10,000,000 because the impact would be less serious on each person. With a single lender, such a huge default would definitely take the lender under.

Bonds are considered to be quite conservative as investment options, mostly because the possibility of losing one's money is way low. Short of going out of business, bond issuers repay their debt obligations in full, and even in the event of going bankrupt, bonds are treated as creditors and paid first from the liquefied assets of a company. Governments absolutely pay their bonds, sometimes issuing a new bond just to repay the old.

Characteristics of Bonds

While there are quite a number of types of bonds, some of their characteristics are uniform to them all. Understanding the characteristics and terminologies used to describe them is crucial to learning how to invest in them.

The *face value* is the principal amount that the issuer is expected to pay the holder of a bond when the period that has been agreed upon passes. The face value remains fixed over time even when the supply and demand drive the price up in the stock market. These external influences of the stock market determine whether the bond sells at a premium (higher than the face value) or a discount (lower than the price indicated on the bond certificate).

The *maturity*, of course, is the due date for the bond's principal. The issuer decides the maturity period for the bond, and the market responds by buying into the idea with their money. A lengthy maturity time increases the risk of non-repayment, so the issuer has to promise a higher yield to entice investors.

At the time of issuing the bond, the borrower promises to pay a certain amount over the face value, which is otherwise known as the interest rate or the *yield/coupon*. The coupon is the equivalent of servicing a loan, with the borrower expected to pay a certain amount every year or semi-annually. This coupon could be fixed (which means that it never changes despite the state of the economy), or it could be adjustable, allowing the borrower to vary their coupon payment depending on certain market conditions.

Because their interest rates are either fixed or more rigid than the rest of the stock market, bonds are considered to be a safe haven for conservative investors during an economic crisis. Lower interest rates in the general economy drive the interest of a bond higher due to increased demand. The increased demand comes about because investors suddenly view bonds as being more profitable even if their price remains the same. Bond yield thus moves in an inverse direction with interest rates in the rest of the market—down when the former is high and high when it is low. Another factor that affects yield is the rate of inflation. With their low-interest rates, bonds become attractive when the inflation rate is lower because the net yield increases. Short-term bonds that are expected to be exposed to a shorter period of inflation tend to have a lower interest rate while those with a longer maturity period (and thus risk) require a greater interest in recompense.

Based on the yield, we have several types of bonds. The common one is the coupon bond where the issuer pays a certain amount of money above the face value of a bond. Another type of bond is the *zero-coupon* type, which is issued at a discounted rate compared to the face value. When the bond matures, the bond is paid in full, and the investor makes their money that way. The United States treasury bills are traded as zero-coupon bonds, so a $100 note sells at, say, $98. At maturity, the inflation-adjusted interest rate will be around 2.5%.

Another type of bond is the *convertible* type. This one allows bondholders to take the decision to convert their bond principal and use it to buy stocks. The option to convert debt into equity when the share price reaches a certain level allows private bond issuers to reduce the coupon. The lowered interest rate at the point of issuance serves the company better as the project takes off, and the fact that the debt is converted into equity dilutes the stakes of other shareholders at no cost to the company. As for the investors, the convertible bond presents double insurance for their investment. If the share does not reach levels attractive for purchasing, the bond yield is still high enough to give a considerably good return. But the fact that they can convert the bond into stock at any time, at any stock price, means that the investor gets their pick of the best moments to buy shares, which could be very profitable.

A similar but somewhat different type of bond is the **callable** type that may be redeemed by the issuer at any point before the maturity. The callable bond allows the issuer to buy back the debt at lower interest rates and re-issue at a cheaper cost. Because issuers buy the bonds back when interest rates are in decline, it means that the bondholders are relieved of their bonds at just the point when the price is in an upward trajectory. For that reason, investors do not overly like callable bonds and opt for non-callable types when the coupon rate, maturity, and credit rating of the company is the same.

Bonds Issuers

The three main types of entities issue bonds are corporate, municipals, and governments. The government is the main bond issuer, responsible for more than 50% of all bonds floating around in the stock market. Bonds that are expected to mature within the year are defined as bills, those that mature within ten years of being issued are known as notes, and those that are expected to mature ten to twenty years after their issue are known simply as bonds. The more conventional name for all three categories of government-issued bonds is treasuries. It is not uncommon to hear them all being referred to as treasury bills, treasury notes, and treasury bonds respectively.

Because these bonds are unfamiliar and investors are often unsure whether the issuer can actually pay up, the coupon income is often specified as being tax-free in a bid to attract more investors.

Comparison with Stocks

Stocks represent a stake in the business while a bond is essentially a credit service an investor extends to the company or the government. The only reason corporate entities and governments issue bonds is to raise money while stocks may also be issued to comply with government regulations. While the money raised during an IPO goes a long way to boost the company's operations, it is often held as liquid assets because an IPO is simply a matter of a business going public to increase its legitimacy and boost public confidence in its products. An initial public offering is a statement that a company is past the start-up stage. A bond issue means nothing more than that a company needs money for operations and wishes to borrow.

Another area where stocks and bonds differ is in maturity. While bonds come with a pre-arranged maturity date, stocks are perpetual. One can hold on to a stock for as long as they wish, collecting dividends on their investment for as long as a whole century. The longest maturity time for a bond is about 30–50 years.

The way that investors make money from either a stock or a bond also differs. With a stock, the price appreciates over time, raising the purported value of an investment (the money a person would make if they sold their shares at this exact moment). This rise is determined by the laws of demand and supply, such that when the market perceives the company as being healthy financially, the price rises because there is greater demand. The opposite is true when the company is struggling financially and enjoys no confidence in the stock market.

From an investment perspective, stocks and bonds differ in one key area, and that is the perception of security for them both. A stock is viewed as a volatile investment because its price is likely to drop at any time. Even though the overall interest rate of publicly traded companies maintains the lower double digits levels, some perform very badly and often go into the negative for protracted periods of time. This volatility makes it extremely hard to predict the return that an investment will bring. For a bond, the interest rate is predetermined and mostly fixed. A bond is considered to be safe and conservative, bringing a stabilizing effect to an investment portfolio. Stocks, on the other hand, come with high risk and high reward and tend to make a portfolio substantially more unpredictable.

Chapter 3: Online Trading Account

Step 1: Determine Your Risk Capital

Answer these important questions:

- How much do you want to use for your swing trading business?

- How much do you have as risk capital?

The amount of money you want to use for trading must be less than or equal to your risk capital. Your risk capital is money that has no living expenses attached to it. It is not meant for any debt repayment and it is not any money held in your retirement savings. You are free to use it for investments and you can stand to lose the money (even though that is not your goal). If you cannot afford to lose the money you want to use for swing trading, please do not proceed further. Forget the idea of trading until you have enough risk capital.

Step 2: Choose a Broker

You do not trade the stock market from your bank account. You need someone who is licensed or a licensed agency called a stockbroker to do that for you. A stockbroker is an individual who is a professional at buying and selling stocks, commodities, shares, and other securities for retailers like you and for institutions or companies. A stockbroker does his or her business of buying and selling via stock exchange and sometimes over the counter and is paid a commission or a fee.

There are several online brokers all seeking for your attention. Your money is important to them, and their platform is important to you. You actually need them in order to trade stocks. But here's the thing: not all brokers are the same in terms of service delivery and their fees. Nevertheless, let me quickly show you the different types of brokers.

Money Managers

These types of brokers handle everything for you – your trades, portfolio, etc. They give you updates on all aspects of your trading. The catch here is the management fees and the initial startup capital. Many of them charge very high fees and their initial investment may be in the range of $100,000 and above.

Full-Service Brokers

In addition to offering you stock buying and selling services, these types of brokers also offer you several plans regarding retirement, plus other investment advice. They provide awesome guidance about what stocks to trade. They are suitable for you if you intend to go into long term investments. Their fees are also on the high side compared to short-term brokers.

Discount Brokers

These are the brokers that are more suitable for swing traders or short-term traders. Their commissions and fees are a lot cheaper than the full-service brokers. You pay them and they buy or sell for you, period.

Choose Online Brokers with Reliable Platforms

In choosing an online discount broker, be sure to scan through several options before making your final choice. Some factors to consider are how responsive the brokers are to your needs and whether their platform is reliable and well-known. Some of the renowned online brokers are Interactive Brokers, E-Trade, Trade Station, Fidelity, TD Ameritrade, Scottrade, Charles Schwab, and Option House.

Check Minimum Balance

Equally, before choosing a stockbroker, you should consider the minimum balance required to open and maintain a trading account with them. In some cases, when your trading account balance drops below the minimum balance, either due to loss or some other factor, some stockbrokers will charge you for a low account balance. So be sure to check several brokerages and compare fees, requirements, etc., before making your choice.

Web-based versus Direct Access Brokers

Online stockbrokers are categorized into those who offer trading through a web browser, and those that require you to download third-party software.

With a web-based stockbroker, you can simply log into the broker's website and enter your buy or sell order from your web browser. However, note that you may encounter quite a bit of delay with filling your orders because it may be routed through a third party.

The direct access brokers give you access to a market maker or ECN (Electronic Communication Networks) through an app. There is no interference from the brokers; you are dealing directly with the stock market. So, you get to control the routing of your orders to the exchanges you wish to use. You have to download trading software apps for you to be able to execute trades directly. You will be charged fees and commissions, plus you may also be billed for access to ECN. If you choose to use direct access brokers, ensure that you check with your particular broker to know what their fees are.

Step 3: Setup Your Trading Account

After you have determined which stockbroker to use, the next obvious thing to do is to set up your trading account with them.

Sign Up

Go to the stockbroker's website and register or sign up to create a new trading account. The option to do this will be displayed as either "register," "signup" or "create account" in a conspicuous space on the stockbroker's homepage.

Documentation

Depending on the stockbroker, you will be required to enter a number of personal information during your registration processes such as your name, address, means of identification, and other personal information. You may be required to scan some documents too.

Deposit Money into Your Trading Account

Obviously, you will need to make a deposit into your trading account before you can start trading. Use electronic fund transfer or any other form of deposit provided by your stockbroker to fund your newly created trading account.

Tour the Platform

Get used to the trading platform by taking a tour or browsing through the features of the platform. Do not rush into trading simply because you have deposited money into your trading account. Get acquainted with the tools and the various pages on the platform first. Practice using the tools in a demo trade so that you are sure what each option means and how they are used in real money trade.

Analyze Stocks

Use the knowledge you have acquired so far to search and analyze stocks. Remember all the cautions and warning you have read in this guide as you determine your first trade.

Trade

When you are ready, enter your first order.

Congratulations! You have successfully made your first order. What matters is that you have followed through and have the guts to put your knowledge into practice. Whatever the outcome of your trade, be sure that you will have a lot of other trades to make and learn from.

Chapter 4: Guide to Investing in Stocks

Without a proper guide, all that information you have gained from reading through this instructive book would be for nothing. In this chapter, we will compress and expand on all the investment guidelines hinted at in earlier topics and provide you with an authoritative and practical guide to investing in stocks—the things you need to keep in mind and the exact order of actions that any investor hoping to establish themselves in the stock market ought to follow.

What comes first? What follows that first action? The activities described here are ordered as they are for maximum efficiency. They comprise of a three-step process that starts with the preparations you need to make before starting your investment journey, followed by the actual investment procedure, and ending with the follow-up activities you need to do to ensure that your investment flourishes. Thus ordered, it makes up for a complete guide to investing in stocks aimed at setting you off on your investment journey with the proper skills and capabilities to ensure profitability in the long run.

Laying the Groundwork

Before you start investing, it is important that you define your objectives and investment goals based on your current capital endowment. From there, you will then decide what style of investing best suits you. To make both of these decisions, you will need to build your knowledge bank.

Build Your Knowledge Bank

A wise investor is a wealthy investor. Knowledge is the most important asset an investor accumulates before putting down the money for their first investment. Good investment strategizing comes from having a good grasp of not just financial markets and what sends prices rising and dropping; it also requires that you have a proper understanding of investment strategies and all assets available for you to invest in. Lack of knowledge in the ins and outs of the stock market can have a debilitating effect on an investor. On the other hand, sufficient information, even when it is just theoretical, is a huge boost of confidence. Investors who have a good idea of how people make money in the stock market are more likely to succeed in the stock market themselves because they are exposed to all the strategies that others before them have accumulated.

On the other hand, acquiring even a rudimentary cache of knowledge of investing is assured to put you way ahead of contemporary investors who just put their money in the so-called "hottest" stocks. And the good thing about knowledge acquisition is that it comes in handy whether you are starting your investment journey at the age of 26 or 62. The deeper you go in your learning of the ropes, the more chances you stand for becoming an outstanding investor.

To build your knowledge bank, you will need to gather information from research, reading financial books, observing the masters of the game, and following the market very keenly.

Learn Research Skills

The first rule of investing in stocks is to invest only in companies that you understand. You will need thorough research to understand the current state of the stock market, rising trends, and future projections. Research skills are crucial not just to the actions you will carry out in this practical guide but also later in your investment journey as you pick assets to buy and determine the best buying and selling points for each one of them.

By learning to research, you unlock every successful investor's catalog of investing stratagems and tricks. Research skills are very handy as you lay the groundwork for your investment journey, when you start the real process of investing, and afterward as you keep your portfolio balanced. In the preliminary process, your research skills will help you to learn, among other things, what information is needed to become a good investor. As you select the stockbrokers with whom to open a brokerage account, research skills will also be very handy. You will also need to have polished research skills as you conduct the due diligence analysis of prospective stocks and other assets to put in your stock portfolio.

The good thing about having technology in our hands is that research skills often entail a simple Google search and bookmarking a few articles for later reference. But people often neglect even the simple act of reading the Wikipedia article of the company they are thinking about buying stocks in. As a tip for those exhaustive online searches, use a PC if one is handy. Some of the most informative articles you will find about a critical topic will never make it into the search results of your mobile phone browser.

Read

Reading investment books may be the hardest method of adding to your knowledge bank. But the information that you gather from investment books goes a long way in building your investment skills. Books written by investment legends (a biography, for example) would be especially indispensable because investors will usually share information about their own investment journey, including the mistakes they made along the way. You can then avoid these mistakes in your own investment career and possibly save yourself a fortune.

Books actually make up for a short course you take on whatever topic they are about, giving you comprehensive information on various subtopics. And neither should your readership be limited to books written about the financial markets specifically. Read up, too, on other skills that could come in handy in your portfolio management, such as accounting and bookkeeping. These skills come in handy in the investment process as well as out of it—other areas of your life.

Mentorship and Mentor Study

While researching and reading allow you to gather information about different steps of the investment process, mentorship entails learning specifically from the more successful investors, often those who have achieved the same kind of objectives as you want to achieve or beat the odds you face in your investment journey. Mentorship also acts as a guiding hand to steer you along on your path to establishing a career in investing, informing you exactly what you need to do at every step of the way. Financial advisors make for great mentors (albeit charging ones) in this particular process. In the event that you don't want to spend on a financial advisor and don't have an investor whose brain you can pick as you start off, reading and researching can be just as authoritative as a form of mentorship as the first two.

Mentor study entails watching, reading, and following the investment strategies of master investors. With social media, investors like Warren Buffet, Peter Lynch, George Soros, and others, usually have Twitter handles and Facebook pages where they post their two cents about every topic in the field of investment. Speaking engagements and televised interviews, most of which may be found on YouTube, also provide a treasure trove of information. Books are another source of mentor study. Book writers are usually investing maestros themselves or enterprising people who conduct rigorous research to present the facts and information about investing to you in an accurate and informative manner.

You can also find help through online forums where you get the opportunity to interact with fellow investors and get all your questions answered. Some of the most recommended online forums include Trade2Win and Elite Trader. However, you should vet the participants in these forums carefully, taking care to only listen to contributors with a reputation for professional and profitable investing.

The good thing about all these sources of information is that you are always free to add your own insights and ideas. So, don't be afraid to copy, even tactic for tactic, the strategy followed by a mentor. If your hunches prove to be well-informed (and they are likely to be because you will have the leisure of studying your mentor's investing style objectively and spot any mistakes), you will probably end up making fewer mistakes than they did.

Learn to Follow the Market

When buying assets for your investment portfolio, timing the market is one of the most futile things you can ever do. But in building your knowledge bank, analyzing the market comes in very handy when analyzing how the stock market reacts to different stimuli. Following the market improves your understanding of it because, after all, observation is one of the most useful skills in building knowledge.

Financial news services, such as the Wall Street Journal, Bloomberg, Yahoo! Finance, and Morningstar, among numerous others, are practically indispensable for a new investor hoping to understand the stock market. You will be able to identify the most profitable sectors of the economy, making it easier for you to make the decision on what stocks to buy when it finally comes down to it. Following the market is the only way to identify trends as they form, stay updated on emerging business concepts, and learn more about general business practices and their impact on profitability.

Television is another great way to broaden your knowledge base. Apart from the jargon (which is also good to learn), analysts on TV teach you how to anticipate market reaction to geopolitical, economic, and public relations events. Of course, at some point, you will outgrow the rather shallow and junky analysis, but in the beginning, they could be a treasure trove of information.

Define Your Investment Style

After building your knowledge bank substantially and gaining a deeper understanding of the stock market in general, it is time now to narrow the focus down to your own investment. Everyone has the style of investing that best suits their needs and their personality. Risk-takers need an investment strategy quite different from risk-averse people, and those who treasure balance would like to combine aspects of both. In this step of your investment journey, you start thinking more about the exact ways that you are going to invest.

Vision Statement

A vision statement gives you the chance to define exactly what you are looking to achieve in monetary rewards. The rest of your investment journey is reliant on your ability to define your investment vision statement because this is the point where you factor in your goals (reasons for saving up through investment) and plot out the best route to follow to get there faster and with minimal risk. When defining your vision statement, establish exactly how much money you are looking to have at the end of your investment and how much time you have to raise it. From this assessment, you can determine the kind of investment strategy that will enable you to achieve your goal.

A popular vision for investing is the 25× goal, a dividend stock-investment strategy for people with visions of early retirement that stipulates that you should invest in stocks that pay you enough dividends to match your annual salary. So, assuming that the stocks in your investment portfolio give a dividend payout of about 4% and with $50,000 as your annual salary, you'd need to invest 25 times of that, which comes to $1.25 million to make exactly what you make now. All dividends and any additional savings go toward boosting your investment portfolio, buying more dividend stocks to increase the dividend payout, which is then reinvested for even greater yields.

Factoring in any possible future promotions (and the accompanying raise) and rising expenditures as you accumulate more responsibilities and develop more refined tastes, $50,000 a year will probably be too little twenty years from now. You will probably need $60,000–75,000 to maintain your current lifestyle, adjusting for inflation. You can solve for that discrepancy easily. Just factor in the desired annual dividend payout, calculate with the average yield and find out how much more you will need to have invested. The best thing about the 25× goal idea is that even when you finally start living off your investment, it will still leave your principal intact.

Investment Strategy

With the overarching determinant being your investment goals, your investment strategy is influenced by two main factors—the amount of risk you think you can shoulder and the kind of investor you would like to become in terms of active participation.

Based on risk tolerance, you can be a conservative investor, an aggressive one, or a moderate one. Aggressive investing produces massive profits very fast, and it is suitable for investors with huge goals and a short period of time to pursue them. The risks are rather massive, but then so are the rewards. Conservative investors opt for low-yield investments that are low in risk. Even though this strategy could be quite profitable over the long term, it could also make your investment a very unprofitable venture. Going for the most conservative investment opportunities also means that the chances of missing out on amazing investment opportunities also increase substantially. The balanced strategy is for those investors who want the best of both worlds—medium returns at average risk.

Based on participation, you can either be a passive investor or an active one. A passive investor invests and forgets all about the investment. They don't bother much with price fluctuations and such "trivial" matters. If you want to have the confidence to invest in a stock and forget about it (watch the money flow, as it were), then make *thorough background research* your friend. This way, you won't be worried that your portfolio is losing value because of a stock you picked. Active investors are a whole other breed altogether. More suited to day trading than long-term investments, active portfolio management nonetheless produces great profits.

Investment strategies ultimately come down to the choice of assets that an investor puts in their portfolio. Aggressive investment strategies call for massive growth stocks with high risks and price volatility, a balanced approach seeks out medium growth rate stocks, while conservative investors prefer the tried and tested stocks whose core business faces absolutely no risk of collapse. Active stock investing gravitates more toward the aggressive style, while conservative investing is often passive. Conservative stocks tend to belong to old companies that have established themselves. The opposite is true for aggressive stocks, whose companies are much younger and require a steady hand to halt any possible loss of investment from price volatility.

Action

Having established your priorities and set your investment goals and strategies, it is high time you open an account and get down to the real investing. It is during this phase that you will pick the asset that will go into your investment portfolio. But first, you will need to open a brokerage account.

Open a Brokerage Account

To invest in the financial markets, you are going to need a broker to carry out your buy and sell orders. You should be very careful when picking out your brokerage because even though their only job is to facilitate your investments in stocks, bonds, investment trusts, and the money markets, not all brokers are created equal. There are those that facilitate your investment and do nothing more (discount brokers), and then you have the ones that throw in some sound investing advice into the deal (full-service brokers). A rising trend in brokerage account holding is the robo-advisor type of account where an automated system helps you set goals, buy stocks, and transact. Your choice of brokerage account will be determined by the amount of control you desire.

Discount Brokerage Accounts

Discount brokers carry out your buy/sell orders at a very low price. A discount brokerage account is the ultimate do-it-yourself investment account. Other than some basic information and price comparison tools, discount brokers offer investors virtually no guidance on investment strategizing, whether in the preliminary stages or later on as you manage your investment portfolio. The discount broker is a relatively recent development in the stock market. Previously, only the full-service broker existed, serving the rich because only they (with their deep pockets and huge investments) can afford their services. The discount broker opened up the stock market for people with less capital to participate.

One of the most outstanding discount brokerage accounts is TD Ameritrade. The firm offers great price comparison and analysis tools. Even though you will get no real investment guidance from a person sitting across the desk or on the other side of the phone, with TD Ameritrade, there will be enough information that you may not need an advisor anyways. If you created a good investment objective and came up with the correct strategy, then you probably won't miss these services anyways.

Full-Service Brokers

A full-service brokerage account entails more than the execution of just buy/sell orders. A wide variety of services, such as taxation advice, research tools, financial guidance, and retirement planning, are offered along with the usual execution of your buy and sell orders. The commission charged by full-service brokers eclipses that of discount ones a few times over. The advantage is that you need not get tied up with research, stock selection, and portfolio management.

Because full-service brokers tend to be more traditional and well-established, they tend to have a few benefits that discount brokers don't. For one thing, a full-service brokerage firm is more likely to have a direct link to IPOs, preferred stocks, and other glamorous opportunities. In the same manner, they tend to put together their own investment products, such as ETFs and mutual funds, giving investors an even wider range of investment opportunities to take advantage of.

Robo-advisor Accounts

The robo-advisor brokerage account is the rave in discount stock trading right now. In a few short steps, robo-advisors allow you to create a portfolio of diverse investments and manage these investment opportunities. Robo-advisors use technology to bring together the best features from full-service and discount brokerage to create an outstanding investment vehicle for the average investor. With little more than your personal details, investment goal, and risk tolerance, a robo-advisor creates a portfolio for you and administers it, performing such mundane tasks as rebalancing with little input from you. Keep updating the details and objectives to ensure that the account still reflects your needs. Other than that, investing using a rob-advisor is a pretty hands-off approach to investing.

Even though robo-advisors do not offer the deep house services of full-service brokerage firms, such as special investment opportunities, the wealth management tools are right up there with the best. The three features that make a robo-advisor account such an attractive opportunity for an investor include (1) low upfront investment, (2) great options, and (3) inclusive portfolio management. Moreover, robo-advisors are completely unbiased, making recommendations based solely on your investment goals. The conflict of interest that comes from financial advisors pushing preferential investments to their clients is totally eliminated. The requirements to open a robo-advisor account are also pretty relaxed, which means that you can start investing with as low as $500. Numerous robo-advisor account providers have come up in the past one decade or so, including Betterment, Schwab Intelligent Portfolios, Wealthfront, and SigFig, among numerous others.

With a brokerage account open, the only thing left to do is pick your investments. The options available to you include the 401(k) plan, the individual retirement plan (IRA), and of course, the stocks, bonds, and other assets that you can invest through a brokerage account.

401(K) and IRA Plans

The 401(k) plan is every employee's birthright to the world of investment. It allows you to save for your employment in the most productive way possible—with incremental returns. The contributions to the investment portfolio are also automatic and tax-deductible. A clause stipulating exactly when you will receive full access to your funds is another advantage of 401(k) plans—it allows you to plan for your own investment.

Whatever amount you decide to contribute to your 401(k) plan is taken out of your pay slip before you get the money, which means that your taxable income reduces substantially. As an investment that matures upon retirement, a 401(k) comes in very handy in addition to any other personal investment plan you may have going if your goal is to retire early, like if your investment vision is based on the 25× goal.

An IRA plan allows you to save for huge future cash expenditures, such as retirement, house buying, a car, college fees, etc. There are a few versions of the IRA plan available, including the traditional, Roth, SIMPLE, and SEP versions.

The Stock Market and DRIPs

With a brokerage account, you can take greater control of your investment career in the stock market, picking just the right stocks to invest in. Unlike the IRA and 401(k) plans, you can withdraw from your brokerage account at any time you so wish. The stocks you pick to put in your investment portfolio should pay you a dividend, which you can then reinvest through dividend reinvestment plans for even greater rewards. Shares bought using DRIPs are substantially cheaper because no commission fees are paid in the purchase. Even though you can only cash them out by selling them off to the issuer, they present a great investment opportunity you simply cannot stand to lose.

While picking the right stocks, ETFs, bonds, or trusts, you should bring your research skills to bear and look for the following: the form 10-K, the Form10-Q, proxy statement, annual reports, and statistical data for the last five to ten years.

Form 10-K is a filing that every company does with the SEC, detailing their financial performance for the past year. Other than the audited financial reports (which are very important), the Form10-K also includes the compensation structure for senior managers, subsidiaries held by the company, and the organization structure. All these details are crucial for an investor vetting a company to decide whether or not it is a good investment. Form 10-K is filed by every company, publicly traded or not, with a net worth of more than $10 million or more than 2,000 shareholders.

The Form10-Q is a shorter-term version of the 10-K, filed every quarter. With the information contained in the 10-Q, you can assess the financial performance of a company in the most recent quarter and compare it with previous filings to determine the direction of the company in terms of profit-making and return on investment. The stock price is more responsive to the 10-Q form because short-term investors and traders keep a lookout for it, but as a long-term investor, it simply breaks down the facts already absorbed from the 10-K.

The proxy statement is all about the board of directors, auditing procedures, compensation for senior executives, and voting procedures for stockholders.

The annual report contains the financial repertoire for the most recent full financial year. It also contains remarks from the board of directors and senior management, whereby they comment on the current state of the company and speculate on the future. Because these are people responsible for the day-to-day operations and long-term strategic planning for the company, their views are invaluable for any long-term investor who wishes to get reassured about the security of their investment.

The numbers don't lie, so the saying goes. Having an accurate picture of a company's past performance will give you greater confidence as you decide whether or not it would be a worthwhile investment. And because the past is the most accurate predictor of the future in business, look at the statistics a company has posted in the last ten years or so. If this information is hard to come by, some brokerage firms and financial services companies would only be too willing to share them with you (at a fee). The data you need includes the income statement, the balance sheet, and cash flow statement, all going back five to ten years. Pore over each and every one of these financial statements before making the decision to buy.

Follow your investment strategy to determine the capital allocation for every class of assets.

Follow Up

After buying up a few assets and establishing your investment portfolio, the only thing left to do is manage it. Depending on your cash, you can start with a single asset or a whole group of them. If you were able to buy a few assets and make a portfolio from the word go, balancing it becomes the next biggest thing. If you have monthly or annual contributions, you will also have to invest these new monies very carefully so as not to mess up with your investment strategy. It is important that you ensure that any new assets do not disturb your risk tolerance. If you start with a single asset (e.g., a stock, ETF, or bond), any new monies should go toward buying more assets until you have the desired portfolio.

The way to win the investment game is to look at it as a long-term engagement, with any gains made being reinvested back to enhance the compound interest earned. Your strategy of investing (conservative, balanced, or aggressive) is completely up to you. After analyzing your risk tolerance and investment objectives, you pick the strategy that you feel will be the best one in helping you attain your goals. But on deciding what style of portfolio management you will go with, there are a few things that you need to consider.

With the passive style, you hold back and largely let your portfolio run itself, balancing it only once every year. You get very little control over this strategy. With the active approach, you constantly tinker with your investments based on market direction and trends in the world of investing.

Here, we propose a third approach to portfolio management, one that is more nuanced and, like the balanced strategy of investing, takes the best of both extremes for maximum efficiency. A waiting period of six months strikes the perfect balance between the two extremes. With this interlude, you neither interfere with nor neglect your investments.

The robo-advisor performs all the activities mentioned in this guide. But does that mean that a robo-advisor account is the way to go? Hardly. Even though they are cheaper and less time-consuming, robo-advisors are blind to the most dangerous practice in the stock market—herd mentality. Being run by algorithms, robo-advisor accounts tend to respond similarly to market stimulus because there is no human instinct to control them. Studies have indicated that the stock market crash of 1987 (or Black Monday as it is popularly known) was caused by automatic sell orders that rely on the price of other assets, a trait that features prominently in robo-advisory accounts.

Chapter 5: The Risk Involved while Investing in Stocks

As indicated in the chart, the stocks in the S&P 500 have appreciated over 100 times since 1900 (data is purely illustrative).

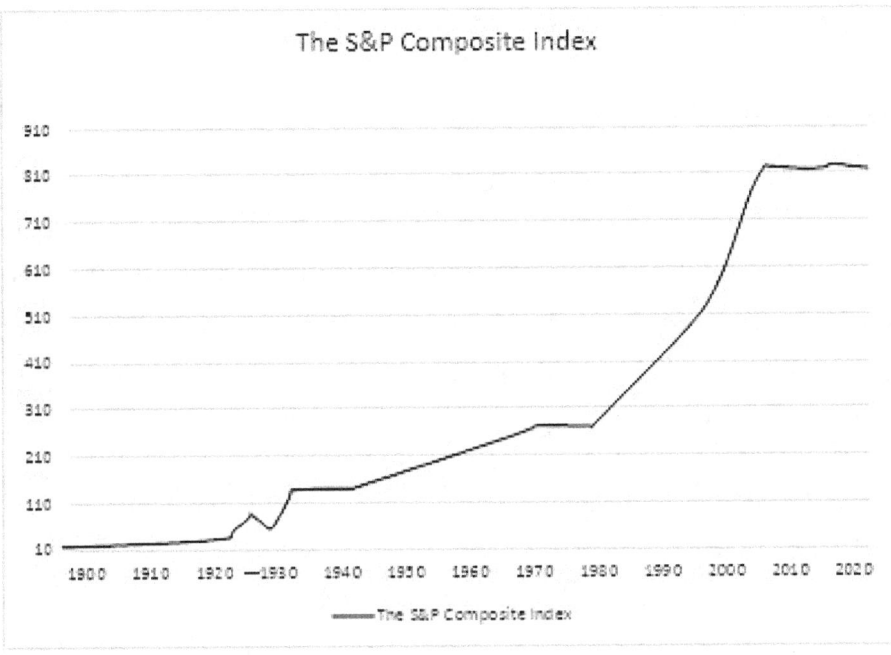

The S&P Composite Index

But where there is a reward, there is also a risk. It is also very possible for you to lose money, which is why you need to be very careful how you pick your stocks and manage them. But you will soon find that there are some risks that you can keep under control and others that are totally out of your control. The only thing you can do in the face of uncontrollable risks is to safeguard your investment against massive losses. And because every investor is always keenly observing the market to spot possible future danger and make a move right now to avoid it, the riskier a situation looks, the more likely it is that a bunch of investors will react to it in a certain way. The concerted actions of investors affect the stock market in a particular manner, which brings about price volatility.

Stock Market Volatility

Risk in the stock market is caused by interest rates, equity prices, foreign exchange rates, and commodity prices. Bonds are also affected by the prevailing interest rate in an economy but in the inverse direction. Higher interest rates drive down demand for bonds and cause an overall lag in the trading volumes of the stock market. As for stocks, the interest rate affects not just the performance of listed companies; it influences the ability of the public and brokerage firms to deal with leveraged stock purchases. A higher interest rate, therefore, spells doom for the whole stock market.

Price risk comes from the volatility of stocks. It is the probability that the price of a stock or stocks in an investment portfolio will fall over a long period of time. The risk of a stock dropping in price can either be systematic or unsystematic. Systematic risk is the risk that occurs across the whole stock market, bringing down the price of stocks in many or all sectors of the economy. Unsystematic risk, on the other hand, affects a single stock or the stocks in a particular industry, like the oil and gas sector when oil prices drop.

The foreign exchange risk affects the price of stocks indirectly through the company whose stock an investor owns. It also affects the profitability of the stock portfolio when it contains a few foreign stocks. The price at which currencies exchange shifts based on the economic performance of that country.

Companies that have foreign operations and move profits home after making them in another country are affected by the exchange rate in bringing these profits back home. When the US currency gets stronger, the conversion of profits earned turns up less money, with the stock market responding by showing less enthusiasm with the company's shares, which brings its price down. For the diversified investor with foreign stocks, any profits earned in another country will still need to be transferred home.

Finally, we have commodity risk, which is the unpredictability of the price of shares that is caused by the changing cost of commodities, such as oil, minerals, agricultural produce, etc. For example, if beef prices rise steeply in the open market, the profit margins of food companies, such as McDonald's, will fall immediately because investors can foretell lower profit margins in six months or one year. When oil prices climb, it becomes more expensive to transport goods, which means that retailers will hike prices, see considerably fewer sales, and post less impressive financial reports sometime later. Anticipating this poor performance, investors will sell, bringing the stock price down. The good thing about commodity risk is that it is very easy not just to mitigate it but also to profit from this risk. While transportation companies and those that rely on them to do business suffer, oil companies will be outperforming their peers. These stocks move in opposite directions with a particular product as the fulcrum balances each other out.

As indicated above, you can neither predict nor control risk. The best you can hope for is to hedge against total loss by maintaining a well-hedged portfolio. With risk comes volatility, which is essentially the rise and fall of stock prices from time to time as investors react to the goings-on.

The foremost cause of risk in the stock market and the volatility that accompanies it is the economy, to which the stock market is inextricably linked. Any downturns in the economy create a corresponding decline in stock market performance. For example, after the economy lost trillions in the dot-com bubble between 2000 and 2002, the stock market went into decline, with all major indexes dropping by significant levels. What happens when the economy is bad is that there isn't as much money for people to invest in stocks anymore. The demand drops—meaning, stock prices fall. People who already own shares, therefore, lose a significant portion of their investment. Even worse, the losses suffered during an economic downturn take time to recover as the stock market adjusts back to its previous position. Not only do you lose money as an investor, but you also lose valuable time when your investment is recovering loses instead of accumulating gains. Foreign stocks come in handy in enabling you to mitigate against risks caused by a downturn in the domestic economy.

Inflation erodes the purchasing power of the currency and eats into any cash reserves a person may hold. Fixed-interest investments, like bonds, are most affected by inflation because unlike stocks, they do not benefit from price adjustments companies do when inflation rises. Whatever the percentage gain an investment provides, the percentage of inflation eats directly into that, so that an investment that produces an interest of, say, 4.5% at 2% inflation gives the investor effective capital gains of 2.5%. The higher the inflation rate, the lower the effective interest rate of an investment becomes. To make matters worse for the stock market, inflation also affects other sectors of the economy. A recession is often preceded by high inflation levels. It causes stocks to rise in price, but it also creates massive volatility.

The stock market is a perfect study in human psychology. When a stock performs well, people flock to buy it, causing the price to shoot up even higher and adding to the belief that it is an attractive investment opportunity. This phenomenon is referred to as market value risk. Trends in the market determine which sector of the economy investors flock and, for that matter, the specific stocks they prefer to buy. Especially when you buy the stock of a company considered as boring and unexciting, you will be exposed to market value risk, with minimal investor interest bringing the value of your stock down and taking a huge chunk off your investment. Market value risk would be a nonentity if it weren't so hard to watch the rest of the stock market growing while your stock flat-lines. In fact, for many seasoned investors, the pains of market value risk present a great opportunity to consolidate their holding in a company. But many investors have also fallen to the temptation to sell and join the rest of the hoi polloi in chasing the next big thing. Spreading your money in a few stocks in different sectors gives you the relief of having at least one stock that is doing well at any one time.

Any time a major economic power suffers a downturn in its economy, other economies feel it too. This is true even for rivals that have little political and cultural cooperation otherwise. China, for example, is a rival to the United States in practically every area, from the financial system (communist versus capitalist) to information and media policies (highly controlled versus free press and information access). The two countries can hardly be called allies. But the economic codependency of the two countries means that any time the Chinese economy slows down, the stock market in America reacts. Case in point, the tariff wars that have been instigated by President Trump have been cited by pundits as one of the reasons why the stock market seems to have slowed down from its bull run that started with the election of Donald Trump. Geopolitics pretty much shape world stability. When Britain votes to leave the European Union, the region becomes considerably weaker as an economic bloc, which means strategic planning by international companies is affected. The stock market suffers. Any maneuverings by hostile world powers against any major military superpower are interpreted by the market as being a possible trigger for war. The stock market suffers.

At the individual stock level, the perception of the public about the state of its issuer is what causes volatility. The job of maintaining a good image in public is very crucial to any traded company. Public relations departments work around the clock to craft an image of their company that is appealing. Any hits and misses in the public relations department, especially for the "hot" shares that everyone is always keenly following, have an immediate effect on the stock price. The news media also contributes to this volatility. When a company is reported to have recalled a product, missed a product release date, suffered a data breach, or suffered any such misfortune, stock prices react instantly.

Risk does not come exclusively from external factors. Sometimes the reason why you lose a lot of money is simply that you were too afraid of losing it to start with. Most of the best investment opportunities you are ever going to find will come accompanied with massive risk. If you cannot overcome your fears and go through with an investment even if there is a chance your stock will drop and lose you some money, you will make "safe" investments in bonds and maybe preferred stocks, where you are assured of getting some returns. In 20 years, you will have doubled your initial investment. Had you taken a little more risk, you could have recouped it three times over or at least two times over if your account for possible losses in the 20-year investment period.

Risk Tolerance

To demonstrate the concept of risk tolerance, let's look at two examples. Richard is a 52-year-old corporate lawyer at a small firm in New Jersey. He has a small family of four, but he is the only breadwinner. With an eye in his life after retirement, he has invested in the stock market for the past 23 years and accumulated quite a fortune on his investment portfolio. And as a seasoned investor, he has seen it all. In fact, he barely made it through Black Monday. The lessons he learned then enabled him to sail easily over the dot-com bubble—even make some money on it. Byron is a 31-year-old programmer from Seattle. He is recently married, with two kids.

Normally, the seasoned, confident investor would be unshaken by this. After all, he has lived through it all. He knows how to work the ropes. The inexperienced investor is more likely to make a cautionary move. But in our special case, Richard systematically sells his high-interest shareholdings and puts the money in the lesser reward bonds market. Byron, the unseasoned investor, studies the market, makes a few strategically placed purchases, and three years later emerges with almost double the principal.

What does our little anecdote reveal about investing in the stock market? It shows that any two investors cannot stomach the same magnitude of risk. Even in the same conditions, with the same opportunities and risks, people will react differently to changes in the stock market. The man who is close to retirement, with his whole life's worth of investments at stake three years to his retirement date, can tolerate a lot less risk than a fresh-faced investor with his whole life ahead of him. To put it plainly, risk tolerance is the magnitude of risk that any investor can tolerate.

Some of the factors that affect risk tolerance include the time you have to keep investing, future work prospects, assets owned apart from stocks, social security funds, and the availability of endowments (e.g., inheritance and trust funds). People who have more of all these things tend to be more aggressive in their investments than those who have little of it. Another reason why an investor might be more aggressive in the face of massive risk is if they are well-versed in the art of investing. With years of investing under the belt, professional investors can invest in stocks that have a risk factor of 50–100% and a similar potential for return without blinking an eye. But even these investors are usually covered by a foundation of carefully accumulated risk-free portfolios.

In the hierarchy of risk tolerance, the daredevils who actively pursue high-risk and high-reward stocks are followed by people with a moderate tolerance for risk. The riskiest stocks moderate risk-takers will accept have a factor of 50%. A diversified stock portfolio comes in handy for people who have moderate risk tolerance.

At the very bottom of risk tolerance is the conservative investor. Conservative investors have virtually no tolerance for risk because the stakes for losing the accumulated gains are higher than those of losing out on a good return. Retirees like Richard fall in this category. The priorities change from the rate of return to liquidity and guarantee for returns.

Assessing Your Risk Tolerance

To assess your risk tolerance, answer the following questions.

What are my goals?

Investing is most effective when you have a perfect idea of what you are accumulating money for. It is even better when you have a solid idea exactly how much money you are going to need or at least a fairly accurate estimate. Based on goals alone, the more the money you need to attain a particular goal, the lesser the risk tolerance you can withstand because it is better to have a fraction of the money you need to achieve a certain goal than lose all your money. With a properly formulated investment strategy and well-defined tolerance for risk, you can then proceed to invest prudently and hopefully make enough money to meet your goals.

How much time do I have?

The timeline between starting your investment journey and the time when you would like to reap the rewards of your investment is very influential in determining the level of risk tolerance you can withstand. A longer timeline means that you can ride out the most volatile upturns and downturns in the market. The stock market recovers from the roughest of recessions in four or five years. For example, after the 2008 stock market crash, the market had completely recovered by 2014. An investor with a portfolio set to be liquidated in 2019 would have had ten years to recover while one who anticipated liquidating their portfolio in 2010 would have had much less time. As you move closer to the time you intend to liquidate your investment, your risk tolerance decreases considerably.

What is my life stage?

The stage you are in life determines the amount of risk you can take. Older people with less time left in their working lives have less risk tolerance than younger people who have yet a lot more time to make more money and invest.

What is the size of my portfolio?

A portfolio that holds $1 million can cushion a loss better than one worth $100,000. As long as the risks are spread around, people with bigger portfolios usually have a higher level of risk tolerance. Investors like Warren Buffett devote millions to each stock investment because he will hardly feel it if a few hundred thousand dollars is lost.

What is my personal comfort level?

Some people are naturally risk-takers while others prefer to stick to the safer route. One way to determine your comfort level as far as the stock market goes is to participate in a mock trading exercise and see how stressed you are when your mock investment is performing badly. If you cannot stand to watch your money diminish as stock prices drop, then you should probably stick to the less uncertain areas of the stock market (e.g., bonds).

The Dangers of Ignoring Risk Tolerance

Not only should you determine how much risk you can stand, but you should also make sure that you have it written down somewhere you are not likely to forget. When you start investing, every investment should be confined to within the safest bounds of your risk tolerance. When you don't factor in your risk tolerance, you are likely to panic and exit from an investment when it is within your risk levels and possibly lose money when it picks up.

Investing requires a certain level of confidence that you cannot achieve without understanding your own risk tolerance. Finding out exactly what your risk tolerance is will give you a proper idea of the kinds of drops in share price you can stomach based on solid considerations discussed above. Even if you are less of a risk-taker, understanding the reasonable levels of risk tolerance suitable for someone with your financial goals, timeline, and portfolio size can embolden you to venture to the riskier sectors where rewards are higher. Similarly, an avid risk-taker will be cautioned by the results of their risk assessment to engage in less risky investments if they are not in a good stage in life for it.

Stock Portfolios

A stock portfolio is an investment tool that allows an investor to put together a collection of assets (e.g., stocks, bonds, mutual funds, ETFs, and commodities). A portfolio is usually a binder, physical or electronic, that is kept in the custody of the owner or placed with a portfolio management firm. The assets placed in the portfolio should be selected according to the investor's risk tolerance, a summary of which should also be kept with the portfolio as an electronic file or print-out.

The consideration for risk tolerance allows the investor to update their portfolio by selling off any assets that no longer align with their investment goals, keeping the portfolio true to their aims and objectives. So, if your risk tolerance is high, your investment style will be aggressive, which calls for a different mix of high- and low-risk assets from the conservative style of investment.

When planning out your portfolio, it helps to think of it as a pie that you can cut into smaller pieces of different sizes. Every piece of the pie represents a class of assets in which you invest to reach a certain goal. Even when considering risk tolerance and other such matters, portfolio breakdown should be done in accordance with the investment objectives and keeping in mind the amount of money you have to invest. Let's say, if you are starting out with savings of $100,000, you may not want to invest it all in one stock or in stocks only. You also want to be sure that the way you distribute your money among the different asset types will give you the returns you need to meet your goals.

As a rule of thumb, the stocks of small-cap companies with high growth potential serve as the foundation for high-risk tolerance portfolios. These stocks may grow over 100% in a few years, but they are also just as likely to collapse and lead to a huge loss. Other high-reward and high-risk assets include large-cap growth stocks, real estate investment trusts, and high-yielding bond issues. On the other end, we have the stocks of large-cap established companies in defensive industries, like retail, agriculture, and health industries. Others include high-grade cash equivalents and investment bonds (bonds issued by corporations or the government for investment, not recurrent expenditure). Combining these two extremes gives a balanced portfolio that gives average returns with medium-level risk.

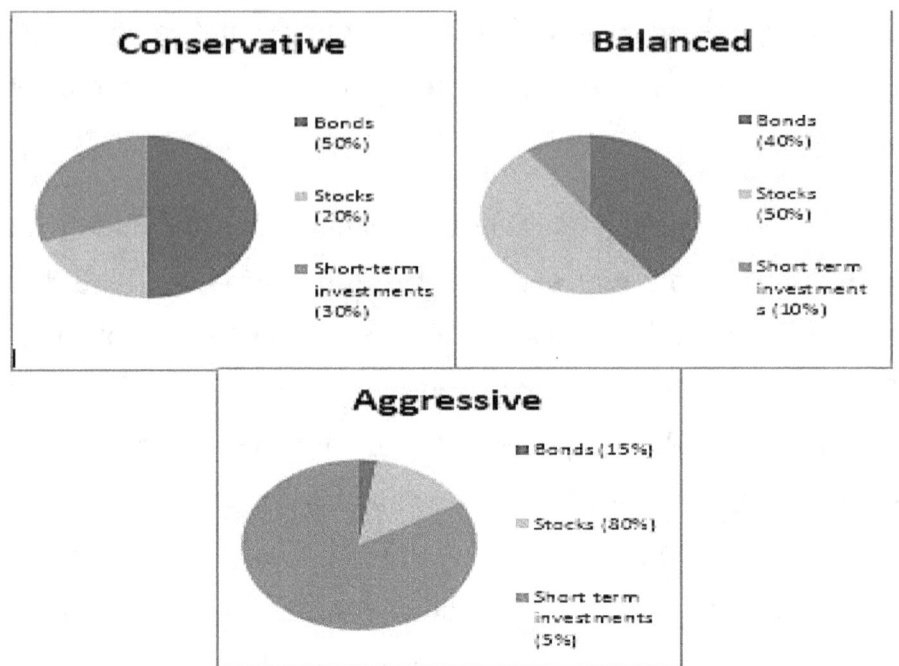

Portfolio Management

Creating an investment portfolio counts for nothing if it is poorly managed because then it does not fulfill its purpose of helping you achieve your investment objectives. Portfolio management entails the whole process of selecting a suitable investment policy. In its most complex form, portfolio management is a finely tuned science that entails determining the best investment mix for you. This format of portfolio management is called active management, and it entails having an administrator who is constantly moving assets around with the intention to outmaneuver the market for the highest possible returns. Active management is best suited for short-term investments of up to seven years or in the last five or so years of a long investment period. The closer control reduces the risk of being caught flat-footed and minimizes risk.

In its simplest form, portfolio management entails simply the process of selecting the most suitable assets for the attainment of investment goals and bundling them together. This more relaxed method of managing an investment is known as passive management. The manager normally just observes the performance of assets and rarely interferes except when absolutely necessary. In passive management, there are no concerted efforts to outsmart the market. A passive style of portfolio management is best suited for long-term investments.

Portfolio management comprises of three elements. The first one is the asset allocation described above. In asset allocation, the investor rigorously vets every stock, index, ETF, REIT, or whatever other assets they intend to invest in before committing to putting their money there. This ensures that no surprising new discoveries spring out later to mess up with the objectives for investing.

The second element of portfolio management is diversification. Diversification is necessitated by the fact that no one can possibly predict with accurate consistency the financial assets that are likely to give a good return and those that will flop. By combining assets from different classes, you can distribute the risk out so that when one asset generates a loss, another one posts a good gain and balances out the loss. We will discuss diversification in more detail below.

The third element of portfolio management is rebalancing, an exercise in realigning one's objectives with the contents of the portfolio. Rebalancing is done once every year in passive portfolio management and as often as possible in active management. While rebalancing, the investor considers gains made throughout the year and ensures that the balance of risky and conservative assets is maintained. For example, investors who decide on a 60/40 mix of high-risk to low-risk assets (because their risk tolerance requires such a mix) will do well to rebalance their portfolio before the higher gains made by the high-risk and high-return assets overpower the lower returns of low-risk assets and warp the balance of the portfolio in favor of high-risk assets. If the gains made by assets are not distributed in accordance with the original plan, the portfolio will soon be more aggressive than balanced.

Diversification

Diversification is a very important strategy for investing. As a financial term, it means simply distributing your investments in various industries for stocks, combining different financial assets, and creating a mix of these assets that will enable you to meet your investment goals. But in the world of investing, diversification refers to a very specific strategy of investment—the careful selection of assets that would react in different ways to a particular event. So far, we have identified the events that create market volatility and make investing in the stock market a risky endeavor. A portfolio combines shares with ETFs, REITs, trust funds, bonds, and other assets, but if not done properly, it can combine assets that react the same way or in a similar manner to events in the economy.

With diversification, you put together stocks that fit together like a cogwheel so that every drop in the price of a particular asset is counterbalanced by a rise in the value of another. When the price of oil stocks goes up, you can almost be assured that airlines, which have to charge more because oil is selling at higher prices, will be doing less business. Their stocks will most probably drop. The inverse is also very true. Having a stock from each sector in your stock portfolio means that your portfolio will always be balanced out whatever happens in either industry. If the oil and airline industries combination does not appeal to you, then you can trade out oil with railway companies. When anything happens to reduce traveler confidence in the airline industry, railroads experience a surge in travelers and vice versa.

Another fantastic combination of assets that can help you keep your portfolio balanced out is that of stocks and bonds in general terms. Stocks normally drop in price when interest rates climb, a time when the price of bonds climbs. Most investment gurus define diversification as simply ensuring that you don't keep all your eggs in a single basket. This hypothetical basket represents the geographical location, economic sector, and investment type.

Pros and Cons

The benefits of diversification have been addressed at length above. The main reason why we diversify, however, is that it allows you to secure your investments against market volatility and keep your investment stable.

By thinking about the risk quotient of assets before choosing to invest in them, we can identify potential hurdles before they become too problematic. For one thing, diversification forces us to think about our risk tolerance, which is the foundation for a good portfolio.

One of the biggest drawbacks to diversification comes from a very curious aspect of the diversification process—choosing your assets. With so many assets to choose from, you might get stumped, unable to choose between different assets.

Another disadvantage of diversification is that it demands that you select stocks from different, unrelated industries. Choosing between a few different good assets in the same market sector leaves the chance that the asset you forfeit is the best one of them all and you can only watch as it rises in price and you cannot take advantage. The opportunity cost of choosing one stock over another could be very demoralizing.

Another con to excessive diversification is that the balancing out of assets in your portfolio whereby a rise in one asset is met by a corresponding drop in another leads to average returns. The cost of trying too hard to ensure that your portfolio will bring you no losses is the fact that you can never make much money. The former hinders the latter.

Another drawback to diversification is that you are more likely to incur massive costs while trying to balance it out by constantly buying and selling.

So, is it worthwhile diversifying? The answer is *definitely!* A diversified portfolio is a huge confidence booster because it assures you that your investment is secure. The only problems arise when you overly diversify or micromanage the risks associated with every asset on your portfolio. Diversification goes hand in hand with portfolio management. The more closely you monitor your portfolio, the better you can diversify. If you think the passive style of portfolio management does not pay enough attention to the assets in your portfolio, a midway point between active and passive portfolio management can allow you to hit the sweet spot between over-diversifying and not doing it thoroughly enough.

Chapter 6: Stock Trading Terms

A/D: Advance/Decline line

ADX: Average Directional Index

Ask size: The sum of the entire amount that is offered at the current ask for selling a particular security.

Ask: The best (lowest) price that is offered to SELL a particular security or stock. Ask means sell.

ATR: Average True Range

Auction Market: This refers to a market where buyers specify the maximum amount, they are willing to buy a stock and sellers indicate the minimum amount they choose to accept for the same stock. When both parties come to an agreed price, a trade occurs.

Average down: Refers to buying extra units of a particular stock that is held by the investor at a much lower price than the initial purchase price. This usually brings about a reduction in the average price that the investor bought the stocks.

Averages and Indices: Use to measure the joint performance of a group of stocks or securities.

Bar chart: Vertical bars used to represent price movements for a specific duration. It is also known as OHLC – Open, High, Low, Close.

Bear market: A market that has a downward trend when averagely measured.

Bid size: The sum of the entire amount that is offered at the current bid for buying a particular security.

Bid: The best (highest) price that is offered to BUY a particular security. Bid means buy.

Black box: Software for trading

Blue chip stock: A well-known stock that is generally perceived as very strong financially.

Breakaway gap: A gap not immediately filled while the price is moving towards it.

Bull market: A market that has an upward trend when averagely measured.

Buy stop: This is an order that is used to buy securities for a price above the current price.

Buy to cover: This is an order that closes a SHORT position. It could be for all or some of the SHORT position.

Buying into weakness: This refers to buying a stock as the price is falling instead of waiting for it to get to its lowest point before buying.

Call option: This refers to an option (not an obligation) to buy commodities, bonds, stocks, or any other financial instrument at an agreed amount within a specified time frame.

Chart analysis: This refers to an analysis that is used to predict which way the next move of a security will go. Analysis of the security's price action like the support/resistance and the highs/lows on a chart are used to make this prediction.

Choppy market: This means that there is no steady or stable movement in the market. It refers to a time when there are quick upward and downward price movements which makes it difficult to see any trend.

Commission: This is the money paid to a broker (a fee charged) for selling or buying securities on behalf of a client.

Commodity: These are raw materials traded on the stock market, for example; oil, silver, or gold.

Correction: This is a short-term decline in price (of at least 10 percent) after a security or stock has previously risen.

Day trading: This refers to the type of trading where all trades are cleared before the close of the market (before the closing bell).

Downtrend: This refers to a period where prices begin to make LOWER highs and LOWER lows. That is to say, the highest price positions are comparatively lower than previous highs, and the lowest price positions are comparatively lower than previous lows.

EMA: Exponential Moving Average.

Equities: These are preferred stocks that represent a share for a company.

ETF: Exchange Traded Funds – a fund that tracks a group of stock and can be actively traded.

Exhaustion gap: This refers to a filled gap after which price moves in the opposite direction of the gap causing a reverse trend.

Expiration date: This is the date that the validity of an option ends.

Extended: This refers to a situation where a stock or other financial instrument has moved very far either upwards or downwards too quickly.

Filters: The rules used by a trader to sift through several trades to determine those that are good and profitable.

Front Month: This is the nearest month for the expiration of an option.

Fundamental analysis: This refers to market analysis or stock analysis that arises from forecasts, news, etc.

Futures: These are contracts meant for buying or selling indexes or commodities at a later date.

Gap: When a stock price opens (usually the next trading day) at a different price than where it closed previously (the previous trading day).

GTC: Good Till Cancel Order. This is an order which remains open until it is filled, or it is canceled. But it expires after 90 days if it remains unfilled or not canceled.

GTD: Good Till Date Order. This is an order which remains open until it is filled or automatically canceled on an earlier specified date.

Hedge: It is a way of guarding against losing your investment. This is achieved by carrying out transactions that counterbalance investments that are already in existence.
Hedge fund: This usually refers to a risk-taking investment company. It also refers to using high-risk techniques to invest in instruments in the hope of making huge profits.

HOD: High of Day. This refers to the highest price for a particular day in which a security traded.

Index: This is the measure of a group of stocks' combined performance, for example, the S&P 500 or the Dow Jones.

Indicator: Formula used for predicting the most plausible direction of a stock or security. This is usually some form of complex calculations based on price and sometimes volume.

Inside information: Information that is meant to be kept away from the public because divulging such information will, in all likelihood, affect the price of a stock.

Insider: Usually, a person who has access to a company's privileged information. Also, an insider can be a person who owns more than 10 percent voting of a company's stock.

Insider trading: This can occur on two sides. On the legal side, it is when an insider engages in trading his or her company's stock and keeps the company duly informed of the trading activities. On the illegal side, it is when an insider trades using privileged or inside information.

Investment advisor: One who gives advice to clients about investment opportunities. He or she may also be mandated to carry out trades for their clients.

IPO: Initial Public Offering. This refers to when the stock of a company was first issued to the public.

Island reversal: This refers to unconnected price actions due to the ups or downs of price gaps that trade below or above the gaps.

Laggard: An underperforming stock or sector.

Liabilities: The debt of an individual or a company.

Limit order: This is an instruction given to your stockbroker to buy or sell a stock or security at a fixed price or a better price.

Line chart: A chart that uses only lines to represent closing prices.

LOD: Low of Day. This refers to the lowest price for a particular day in which a security traded.

Long: This means to own a security. Profit is made from going long if prices increase.

Margin account: This is a type of account that allows a trader to buy stocks using credit from his or her stockbroker. Interests on the credit are charged on the trader's account.

Market capitalization: Also shortened as Market Cap. It is the share price of a company multiplied by the total number of outstanding shares to get the value or worth of that company.

Market order: This is an order to trade stocks or securities at the best current market price.

Momentum: This refers to the speed of price or volume movement.

Net change: This means the difference between the last traded price and an earlier closing price.

Offer: The best or lowest price that a seller of a stock stipulates.

Open interest: This shows all futures or open options that are held by companies or individuals at the close of the day.

Open order: This is an order that stays beyond one day in the market.

Option: This refers to an option (not an obligation) to sell or buy commodities, bonds, stocks, or any other financial instrument at an agreed amount within a specified time frame.

OSO: Order Sends Order

Overbought: This refers to a stock or security that is perceived as being overpriced and traders believe it will soon go down.

Oversold: This refers to a price that is considered too low for a security or stock and will obviously rise.

Painting the tape: This means decreasing or increasing the price of a security to make it look worse or better than it is.

Paper trade: This refers to trading without real money. It is a way to practice trading.

Pattern day trader: Traders who buy and sell stocks and securities over four times per day for over five days.

Penny stock: Any stock that is highly speculative and is priced below $1 per share.

Point and figure chart: This is a chart that is made up of Xs and Os and which plots only according to predetermined price fluctuations.

Portfolio: This refers to the assets, bonds, shares, or trades held by an individual or a company.

Pullback: This is a non-dominant movement that occurs following price movement in a trend's direction. It is a comparatively small plunge in price in a dominant uptrend. It is also known as retrace.

Put option: This refers to an option (not an obligation) to sell commodities, bonds, stocks, or any other financial instrument at an agreed amount within a specified time frame.

Relative strength comparison: This refers to a comparison of a stock's trend with the market to gauge the stock's performance.

Relative strength: This means an index or security is stronger than another.

Relative weakness: This means an index or security is weaker than another.

Resistance: This is a position or a level on a chart where stock prices run into excessive supply (or too many sellers) thereby causing the prices to stall for a while and likely fall.

Retrace: This is a non-dominant movement that occurs following price movement in a trend's direction.

Reversal: This is an abrupt change in the opposite direction of a trend.

Risk/Reward: This means the possible loss as against the likely gain in a trade.

RSI: Relative Strength Index

Runaway gap: This refers to a gap that is not immediately filled up while the stock price is in continuous movement towards the gap.

S/R: Support/Resistance

Seat: This refers to being a member of an exchange. Being a member of an exchange confers certain benefits such as reduced commissions.

SEC: Securities and Exchange Commission. This is the organization that controls or regulates the trade of securities in the United States.

Sector: This refers to a collection of stocks that generate returns from similar industries such as energy, airlines, etc.

Securities: This is usually a certificate that has an attached financial value or proof of ownership of bonds, stocks, or other investment products that can be traded.

Sell stop: This is an instruction to sell a stock below its current price. The instruction or order is activated immediately after the price movement arrives at your specified sell price.

Selling into strength: This refers to selling stock as the price is going up instead of waiting for it to get to its highest point before selling.

Settlement: This means there is a completion in trade or transaction. The buyer receives stocks or securities from the seller and the seller receives payment.

Settlement date: This is a date that settlement must occur.

Shake out: This is a situation where investors, as well as traders, leave a position out of fear only to discover that their fears were not true.

Short interest: This is the total number of stock shares that were borrowed by institutions or individuals and which has to be returned to the lender.

Short selling: This refers to selling a borrowed stock or security based on speculation that the price will fall and then looking forward to buying the stock back at a cheaper price. The borrowed stock or security will then be returned to the lender.

Short: This is the opposite of the long position. It means making a profit from stock prices that are falling.

Sideways market: This is a period in the market where there is no uptrend or downtrend. That is to say, there are no higher highs and higher lows, or lower highs and lower lows.

SMA: Simple Moving Average

Spread: Refers to the difference in the ask and bid of a stock or security.

Stop loss: This is a price level that triggers your exit from a position. You should normally set this when you are entering a trade.

Strike price: The holder of a stock option or security has a right to sell or buy at a certain price. That price is referred to as strike price.

Support: This is a point where falling prices seem to reverse back up or stall for a while due to too many buyers (or demand).

Swing trading: The kind of trading that involves buying positions or selling positions with the aim of holding it for about two days or more; focused on short-term (quick) gains.

Technical analysis: This refers to the analysis of securities with the use of charts and other indicators. Technical analysis helps to predict the direction of price movements.

Thin market: This is a market where the offers and bids are very few. It is a market that is not easily liquid and is very prone to slippages.

Tic: This refers to the minimum spread existing between bids and asks. The spread can be in cents or it can be a dollar.

Ticker tape: This shows trades that are completed.

Time and sales: This shows price and trades including size and time.

Top-down approach: This refers to the three steps involved in the analysis. The first step is to analyze the market in general. The second step is to analyze the various sectors, and the third is to analyze the stocks individually.

Trading session: This is the duration or period where trading takes place on the market.

Trailing stop: This is a stop loss order that is not set at a particular amount but at a certain percentage away from a stock's current price.

Trend: This is a period of relatively consistent price movement either upwards or downwards. That is to say, there are either continuous prices hitting higher highs and higher lows, or a continuous period of prices hitting lower highs and lower lows.

Uptrend: This refers to a period where prices begin to make HIGHER highs and HIGHER lows. That is to say, the highest price positions are comparatively higher than previous highs, and the lowest price positions are comparatively higher than previous lows.

Volatility: Refers to the fluctuation in price. Usually, it is used to mean the instability or unpredictability of price movements either up or down.

Volume: This is the total amount of futures or shares that are traded within a particular time.

Washout day: This occurs when there is high volume at the end of a decline that results in the sellers being washed out. The stock resumes its climb as buyers gain control. This is also called the Flush out day.

Whipsaw: This refers to a situation where a trading signal appears briefly but is quickly reversed and leads to a close of that trade

Chapter 7: Short-Term Investment

So far, we have touched on the long-term strategies of investing and treated the long-term as the only bona fide investment strategy out there. But there exists one other strategy of investing where you can maintain ownership of an asset for a shorter period of time (a few months to several years) and still make some good money. Because they are more sensitive to fluctuations in prices than long-term investors, short-term investors engage in more than twice the number of transactions.

If you need a lot of money for some huge expenditure in two or three years and are saving up, there is no reason why you should condemn your money to a savings account that will only erode the purchasing power of your money. You can engage in short-term investment instead. Even though you may not achieve the double-digit growth rates achieved by long-term investments, you can still earn interest rates well above the bank rates.

Now, is one of these strategies better than the other? The answer varies. Long-term investments allow you to maximize the return on investment over a long time while short-term investments capitalize on the shorter-term ventures. The main difference between holding a stock for a few years and holding it for a decade or more is that, in one, you are exposed to more risks, and in the other, there might not be enough time for your investment to reap maximum benefits.

What distinguishes between these two modes of investment is essentially the length of time a person holds on to an asset after acquiring it. Short-term investments are generally considered to be those that are held for three years or less. By this definition, even day trading falls under the auspices of short-term investment even though it may be referred to in more specific terms as trading. Even though trading is an industry all on its own in the stock market, it is still an aspect of short-term investing—the shortest of all investment durations.

Short-Term Investing Strategies

Short-term investing is considered by many to be no different from trading. In some quarters, the names are actually used interchangeably. But is short-term investment synonymous with trading? Ultimately, short-term investors are locked out from many opportunities that make long-term investing so profitable. Holding a stock for a short time means that you might miss out on dividend payouts and have to rely on the buying and selling points. Unlike long-term investments when you might decide to establish a buying period of up to one year to take advantage of dollar-cost averaging, with short-term investing, the one year could be all the time you have to cash in on your investment. You only have the time for a one-off purchase and a sale later on, so it is imperative that you take the most opportune moment to sell for maximum returns.

Clearly, a different mindset is needed to invest in the short run. With short-term investments, we abandon the strategies of Warren Buffet that have been referenced all throughout this book. A new hero, George Soros, becomes our mentor and inspiration. With a net worth of over $24 billion dollars, Soros is the most successful trader of this age. His holdings only last a few years at most, which is why his advice is perfect for this section.

Investment Management Style

The thing about short-term investing (in case you haven't noticed) is that it is very much like day trading. The only difference is that with short-term investing, you do not limit your buy/sell durations to the six hours when the stock market is open. The duration ranges between a few months to one or two years, depending on the type of stock and your investment strategy. Just like with portfolio management, short-term investors follow two predominant strategies—the active and inert investing. The active investor takes the two or three years they have to invest their money in the stock market and puts it into a few different positions within the duration, trying to beat the market by making numerous small gains on capital invested over and over again. Active short-term investors borrow a lot from day traders in their investment practices, doing everything possible to reduce risk.

The inert short-term investor commits their money of a single position or a few positions that will all be traded once. That is to say, after buying a carefully scouted stock, an inert investor sticks with it for however long they intend to invest. Unless the stop-loss price (which is usually lower than the active short-term investor) is breached, they will only make money on the selling price their stock will produce at the end. The amount of money that can be made in this format is rather limited, but it is the more conservative of the two short-term investment strategies.

Breakout

This single transaction by the greatest short-term investor on Wall Street indicates, in a nutshell, the strategies that work best in the short-term investment landscape: get in low, get out whenever the opportunity presents for maximum profit-making. When planning to invest in the short term, it is more advisable to have an exit price than just to sit and wait, then sell at the end of your intended investment period.

The price at which a stock is bought is referred to as the entry point. It serves as the baseline for your investment and forms what is known as a resistance point. The only time you ever sell below this point is when the stop-loss level is reached (discussed below). Otherwise, you create an exit point by calculating the price at which you will need to sell an asset to make a certain percentage profit. By studying the month-by-month gradual change in the price of a stock, you can anticipate the price it will be trading at in the longer short term (six months to one year) and set your exit point accordingly. But here is where short-term investing differs from long-term: when your target price is reached, you sell. This is because volatility is much more of a risk in short-term trading since you don't have the time to wait for the markets to recover.

Short-term investing is more sensitive to short drops and rises in price. After all, day traders make money on intraday fluctuations in stock prices. As an investor of the short-term, you will have to recognize the buying opportunities that last a few hours when you can buy a stock at below-equilibrium prices. Even if you have to wait for the most opportune moment for a whole year, the fact that you were able to buy at rock-bottom prices means that your profit margin will be larger.

Scalping

Rule number one of long-term investing states that you should never attempt to time the market. When it comes to short-term investing, timing is the only chance you have of making money. With scalping, you set the point at which you will need to make a certain amount of money, factoring in the commission fees and taxation, and sell as soon as the desired price is reached. Unlike breakout selling, which calls for an investor to wait until the price reaches the highest possible price (often close to the release of annual financial results and dividend payout when demand goes up), scalping simply aims to sell as soon as possible, counting on multiple trades to make up for lost profits.

Momentum

In short-term investing, an investor achieves momentum by buying into stocks that they understand thoroughly. With this information, they can then anticipate the trend of stock prices and position themselves to profit. Momentum is quasi-long-term investing because sometimes a person can spot a trend from months or even a few years away. To maximize your profits, you always buy at the lowest possible price. So, if a stock reaches rock bottom price during a single trading session one year before it is set to resurge from an event you foresaw, you can buy and hold on to it until your event transpires. This is the exact strategy that George Soros used to make his $1 billion profit in the UK currency crisis of 1992. He was able to recognize the overvaluation of the pound in the European exchange market, and he knew that the UK could not maintain it at that level. He bought up on the short positions for months, and in the end, he made a profit very few investors ever get to make in their entire investing career.

Pivots

In the short-term analysis of stock markets, a certain trend emerges that enables investors to invest with little fear of making a loss. For short periods of time, prices pivot around a certain point, going higher or lower but returning to just about the same price, before moving on to new pivot levels.

The pivot is calculated as the average price of a stock in a day from the highest, lowest, and closing prices.

$P = (H + L + C) / 3$

Central Pivot = (Highest + Lowest + Close) / 3

From the pivot, another price point to keep a look out for is the resistance. This is a price that the stock hardly ever goes beyond because it is above the book value. Past this price is a second resistance point, which is a point at which the price is likely to plummet below the pivot and into the lower support points as the market shies away from the briefly overpriced stock. As mentioned above, these price fluctuations are more sensitive in short-term investing.

To calculate the first resistance ($R1$), we subtract the lowest price (L) achieved by the stock from two times its pivot point (P).

$R1 = (2 \times P) - L$

The second resistance ($R2$) is calculated by adding the difference between the first resistance ($R1$) and first support ($S1$) to the pivot.

$R2 = P + (R1 - S1)$

This is the price below the pivot that a stock hardly ever breaches. There are actually two supports. The first support price below the pivot is an alarm bell that indicates a possible loss. Some investors make this their stop-loss level, but others wait until the price falls below the second support point to exit in the hope that the price will rise before reaching this level.

To calculate the support levels, we subtract the highest price reached by a stock from two times the value of its pivot.

$S1 = (2 \times P) - H$

The second support is calculated by subtracting the difference between the first resistance and the first support from the pivot.

$$S2 = P - (R1 - S1)$$

Pivots are one of those self-governing human phenomena that are maintained for little other than the fact that traders and short-term investors use them to determine selling points and buying points. As such, prices range within the pivot and the first resistance above and first support below, which also happens to be the range that most traders play within. Whenever the price goes up, increased supply pulls it back down, and when they drop, increased demand brings the prices right back up.

Risk Management

Risk management takes considerably greater precedent in short-term investment than long-term ones because the time available to recover is much more limited. For this reason, investors have designed a number of tools to prevent adverse losses, including stop-loss levels and position size.

Stop-Loss Level

Every investment in the stock market carries with it the risk of losing money when the price drops below a certain level. Based on an investor's risk tolerance, when the price drops below to a certain level, divestment is the better option to holding on to a stock. With this particular tool, an investor simply cuts their losses, electing to incur a smaller loss now than risk waiting and lose even more. Stop-loss is a risk avoidance tool of last resort, saving your investment by allowing you to avoid any more of it. If you don't set a stop-loss level at which to exit, you might lose everything. But if you leave with a small loss but your investment capital secure, then you can make up for the loss in a different investment. Stop-loss employs a system of stop measures: the *sell stop* and *buy stop*. Your sell stop and buy stop act as valves to stop you from losing money in market reversals when the price starts moving in the opposite direction.

With long-term investing, the stop-loss level isn't exactly a huge concern because the money is made in wide margins over decades. With short-term investments, a few cents make a huge difference for a stock worth $10, making it even more important to have stop-loss measures.

Position Size

Position sizes are to short-term investments what portfolio ratios are to long-term investments. Position size helps the investor determine the number of shares they will take on every opportunity based on risk tolerance and investment goals. Every investment position you take represents some measure of risk. Every short-term investment in the stock market requires a position size, which is calculated as a product of total investment value, stop-loss, and risk limit.

For example, with a total principal of $250,000 and a risk limit of 10% on the principal, then you can only use $25,000 on every short-term investment to mature in a few months to a year. If you are buying a stock priced at around $20 and you set your stop-loss at $18, then you are willing to risk $2 per share. With a $25,000 investment, you will have 1,250 shares. This share amount, therefore, becomes your position at a 10% risk.

Mastering Short-Term Stock Investing

To master short-term investing, you will need to balance inert and active management styles. This is the most suitable way of operating in the stock market for the short term, especially when you don't have the time to do it full-time. With the following strategies, you can master the stock market in the duration you have set for yourself to raise a certain amount.

Watch the Moving Average

The moving average is the mean value of a share measured for a few days, weeks, months, or years. It allows you to determine whether, on average, the share is in an upward, downward, or haphazard trajectory. Obviously, an upward trajectory is the ideal position to make your investment. Because your selling point may be within a depression in the price of a stock, go for stocks whose price has been steady or generally steady to reduce the chances that your selling point will come at a time when the stock is selling at a price below your buying price.

Understand Overall Cycles

The fluctuation in the price of stocks follows certain observable patterns. There are points at which investor confidence is high and times when the company falls to perpetuity for a while. The period immediately before a company announces its financial results is very volatile. If there are high expectations for a company to perform well, investor confidence drives the stock price up. The market also responds to the actual announcement. Any negative results cause a plummet in stock prices while positive news bumps the price higher. Interestingly, sometimes, a company is seen as having failed when investor expectations are not reached, even if it made good profits. At such times, the price may drop even if the company remains profitable.

As a short-time investor, your money will be made around the quarterly rather than annual financial results. For short-term investors who have mastered the game, the financial announcements season is the best time to sell. A few months afterward, there is a lull in the transactions, which causes prices to drop significantly. This becomes a great opportunity to buy up and wait again for the season of high expectations and speculations to sell. This strategy is a little risky because a company could post losses just when you needed it to make a profit, boost investor confidence, and allow you to exit at a market high. All the same, it is a better strategy that haphazard buying, especially because it will save you the effort of spending all the calendar year waiting for the moment. The November-April period (financial reports released) is the period of maximum stock market activity while the May-October period sees much less activity.

Get a Sense of Market Trends

It is interesting the number of long-term investment lessons you will have to unlearn when going for short-term investments. In long-term trading, you should ignore trends and focus on fundamental analysis. Fundamental analysis focuses on the strengths and weaknesses of a company that affect its long-term profitability, like management and financial ratios. Ratios (e.g., earnings per share, price to earnings, return on equity, price to book value, and debt to equity) help the investor to calculate whether a business falls within the margin of risk that would make it safe to invest.

With short-term investments, trends are great indicators of opportunity. However, trends rarely last over two years. So, if you were to invest for the long term based on trends, your investment would lose value fast as your trend falls out of style, forcing you to exit the market or risk losing money. But with short-term investments, trends are exactly the price accelerators you need to drive the price of your stock up and give you a handsome return in a year or so.

Selling on the News

As stated above, herding is a failing of the stock market whereby people tend to get the urge to buy and sell stocks at the same time, especially when there is news of a certain kind. A company whose product has done well will prompt a surge of demand while an underperformer will be shunned. Any hint of scandal sends short-term investors into panic mode, prompting a massive sale. Unfortunately, a scandal is something you can do nothing about. A company that cheated the IRS out of millions of dollars in taxes will probably go through a long period of litigation that will drive its stocks to the ground. With your investment position open to just a year or two, you cannot afford to wait out any scandal. You can only be too careful in this case and sell at the first hint of scandal, exiting before the share price suffers too much.

But when it comes to time to sell at your own leisure, wait until the news about your stock is positive. With higher investor confidence, your stock will attract a prime price and bring you a nice profit.

Chapter 8: Make Money with Growth Stock and IPO's

Stock Issuance: The IPO Process

An IPO represents the blowing wide open of the shareholder register, previously dominated by founders, early and angel investors and employees (in those companies where the stock option is an incentive for attracting and retaining employees) to include as many of the public as the number of shares a company offers. The price of a company's stock, especially shortly after the IPO, is determined in part by its book value and the number of people who are willing to buy its shares at a certain price. The higher the demand, the higher the stock price climbs. As a prospective investor in the stock market, it is only natural that you are fascinated by the whole IPO process. After all, the understanding of what goes on behind the scenes of an IPO often determines whether an investor considers the freshly issued shares worth buying or not.

There are several ways for a company to go public, but the Securities and Exchange Commission (SEC), a government department mandated with overseeing the stock market and enforcing fair play rules, follows each and every one of them very closely. The most popular format of public issuance is one where an investment bank spearheads the process.

However, there are other alternative procedures for a company to follow in issuing its shares to the public. They are direct listing and Dutch action.

Investment Bank

A bank-issued initial public offering is a five-step journey from private holding to public trading that is overseen by an investment bank from start to finish. First, the business leaders in a company decide to go public, with the intention of raising money or simply in compliance with government regulations. However, because the offering process is a complicated and tightly regulated process, having a firm that specializes in the stock market can be a very good idea.

Selecting the Bank

The first thing to do in the IPO process is to select a bank to underwrite the whole process. By underwriting, we mean that the bank buys or commits to buy in principle all the shares a company intends to issue to the public and then re-issue them in the secondary stock market.

This is an important role for a bank to play in such a key process of a company's financial maturity, so some due diligence is very much in order. Usually, what a business looks for in an underwriter is reputation. An investment bank with a specialty in a business's line of operation gives it an edge because it is perceived as having a better grasp of the institutional investors who might be brought on board during the IPO.

Talking of institutional investors, they are very critical to the success of an initial public offering for a few reasons. But to understand that better, let us first jump slightly ahead and consider the landscape immediately after a company goes public. A spike in the price is usually expected soon after the

IPO. This is the most effective way to create a stable foundation for a company's shares to take off and increase in value over time. To do this, some companies offer their shares to the public at a point where confidence in their future financial performance is high. The SEC enforces a period of lockdown, where transactions are restricted. This quiet period ensures that market hype does not drive the share price too far above its real value and exacerbate the volatility of the whole stock market. When employees and initial investors start selling to take advantage of the short-term rise in price, the share price often drops drastically because of oversupply. Institutional investors, on the other hand, invest for the long haul. They are unlikely to engage in this kind of maneuverings, which makes the stock more stable. This makes it more important for a business to select an investment bank that can rope in the big fish to increase hype and subscription rates.

Due Diligence

The next process in the investment bank format of IPOs is the performance of due diligence checks and conducting the regulatory filings. As mentioned above, the investment bank assumes the responsibility of getting all the shares a company intends to sell to the public and resells it, acting as the middleman between it and the investors. There are various arrangements that the company can enter with the investment bank on the process.

A firm commitment entails a bank undertaking to buy all the shares and re-issue them to the general public. For an investment bank to agree to this arrangement, it has to be very confident that it will be able to make money on the IPO from the underwriting fees and mark-up of selling at a higher price than what they buy the shares for.

Another strategy is called the best effort agreement, whereby the underwriter speculates the amount of money they anticipate to raise from the IPO. Because there is no assurance that the target will be hit, the bank does not undertake to buy all the shares. Its job is simply to issue the stocks to the public for the company. Nonetheless, the bank is expected to promote the shares to the public and institutional investors.

For IPOs that are too big for one underwriter to handle alone, a syndicate is created, with each member contributing to the pool of money required to purchase the whole issue in full from the issuing company. The bank that raises the largest share takes the lead on the offering, keeping the books and overseeing the more crucial aspects of the IPO for a greater share of the underwriting fees. This way, an investment bank distributes the risk of the IPO to a large group of competing banks.

Even though the agreement a business reaches with an investment bank to take them public is crucial to the IPO, it is not the only important thing that goes on in the due diligence process. In fact, this is the most intricate process of the offering. Important documents are crafted, SEC requirements have to be followed, and some very delicate accounting mathematics has to be done, often with a contracted accounting firm for impartiality. A reimbursement clause protects the investment bank from losses in the event of the issuing company withdrawing the offer midway through the process by stipulating that the expenses are to be reimbursed either way. In a letter of intent, the underwriter commits to the offering process by promising to dedicate every effort to ensure that the shares will perform well in the stock market, including promoting to investment bankers among other promotional efforts. On its part, the issuing company commits to provide all information needed by the underwriter and to cooperate in the whole issuance process.

Other important documents in the due diligence process include the registration statement, which is submitted to the SEC showing the financials, management background, ticker symbol suggested for use in the stock markets, holdings by company insiders, and the legal history of a company. The registration statement filed with the SEC identifies the issued company as a component of the stock market and allows the SEC to keep tabs on their financial, legal, and accounting practices.

A prospectus is drafted for all investors, showing the strengths and weaknesses of a company, as a way of giving every prospective investor sufficient and reliable information about the impending share issue. From the prospectus, investors can speculate on the future of the company and make a better decision of whether to participate in the IPO. Another item created for the investors is the red herring document, which is used during the promotional road shows where the underwriters and issuers promote the impending share issue to the public. The roadshows allow both the bank and the issuing company to gauge interest and demand for the impending share issue, which is important for the next part of the process—pricing.

Stock Pricing

After evaluating the prospectus and verifying that all records are in order, the SEC gives approval for the IPO. The issue date is decided between the SEC, the issuing company, and the investment bank underwriting the process. And on the eve of the effective offering, the issuer and the investment bank sit to decide on the best price for the shares. Haggling on share price often comes down to a few cents per share. With millions of shares and billions in net worth often being the stake, every cent counts.

The price set for the stock during this seating depends on a few factors. The most important of these is the subscription rate for the share. During the roadshows, pre-orders are recorded in the order books. Shares that have been oversubscribed are preferred because this indicates greater confidence in the company's future by the stock market. Another consideration is the price at which the issuing company intended to sell its shares in the first place. In order to decide this, the share price for companies in the same industry is assessed. The issuer may want to have their shares sell at a higher or a lower price.

The stock price is calculated against the amount of money expected to be raised to determine the price of each share. The money a company expects to raise and the share of the company to be issued dictate the number of shares and value of each share on the negotiating table. But in the market, after trading opens up, all that matters is market hype, because this determines the enthusiasm of the market and, subsequently, the prices to which the share rises immediately after the IPO.

Trading

The first day a company trades in the stock market is usually very exciting. Depending on the levels of excitement exhibited by buyers, the price either falls higher or lower than the one that the issuer agreed to with their investment bank. The trend established on the first day in terms of volumes traded and price trend may continue for a while, but restrictions placed by the SEC on trading soon after the IPO somewhat limit the volumes of transactions. As such, it is not until a few months after the initial offering that a stock stabilizes.

The Stabilization Process

The undertaker does not disengage from the sharing process immediately after the stocks start trading publicly. They stick around to provide the market with analysis and expert commentary to boost demand. Other mitigating actions to maintain the stock price at the desired price include batch buying or selling to influence the direction of the price shifts that take place soon after the IPO. During this time, the SEC restrictions on price manipulation are usually suspended to allow the stock to pick up at a price that is more realistic.

Incidentally, it is for this exact reason that it is ill-advised to buy into a company soon after its IPO. The price, immediately after the initial offering, is usually artificially modified, which makes it unpredictable afterward when the laws of demand and supply finally take over.

While complicated, the process of issuing shares through an investment bank presents the issuer with greater control over investor interest and stock price after the IPO. The expert guidance of the investment with the SEC regulations that come with initial public offerings also goes a long way in smoothing the process out. The main disadvantage of using an investment bank is that they charge quite an exorbitant underwriting fee and also make a ton of money on the mark-up between the price agreed with the issuer and what the public ends up paying for the shares. Perhaps it is for these reasons that some companies decide to go directly to the public.

Direct Listing

By listing the company's shares on the stock exchange at the same time that they are offered for purchase by the public, a company skips the process of hunting and negotiating with a bank to take the company public. The company also saves on underwriting fees and enjoys all the sweetness of an oversubscribed stock with a price higher than the book value. However, a company that opts for a direct listing forfeits the advantages of having an experienced Wall Street firm promoting the IPO. The stock price from a stock that has been listed directly starts off rather sluggishly.

The companies that are well suited for direct listings are those that are considerably well known already, offering a product that the public is already well aware of. Even if the institutional investors may not join the fray earlier on, the market buzz for its products more than makes up for the lack of an investment banker. Moreover, when investors show more genuine interest in the stock, the price grows organically, driven by real demand rather than blatant price manipulation. One of the most recent direct listings was the 2018 Spotify Technology SA.

Dutch Auction

A Dutch auction allows the buyers to set their own price for a share. A company approaches investors and requests for the number of shares they would like to buy of their company and their price of those shares, relying on the market perception of the business's financial well-being to set a reasonable price. The highest bid price almost always wins the auction and sets the price of a company's shares. Dutch auctions rely on connections to spread the word and give investors the chance to buy shares.

One of the most iconic Dutch auctions of the twenty-first century is that of Alphabet Inc., Google's parent company. Some other companies like Morningstar Inc. and the Boston Beer Company, Inc. have also helped Dutch auctions, issuing their shares to a selected group of people.

Why Invest in the Stock Market?

There are many reasons why investors, both professional and beginners, choose the stock market as their preferred vehicle for investment. The main reason why people do so, however, is that stocks have a better interest rate than most other investments. Unlike a savings account, money devoted to the stock market makes returns way above the inflation rate—as long as the investing has been done with a bit of skill.

Investment Value

Over the long term, stocks have the highest rate of returns when compared to other asset classes. For example, the Standard & Poor 500 Index (S&P 500) had an average annual interest rate of about 11% from 1928 to 2016. With 11%, the time frame falls somewhere between six and a half years and seven years. For other investments like treasury bills that have an estimated annual rate of return of 3.46%, the time it takes to double the investment comes in at slightly over 20 years! That is a long time difference between two asset classes that are both traded in the same stock market.

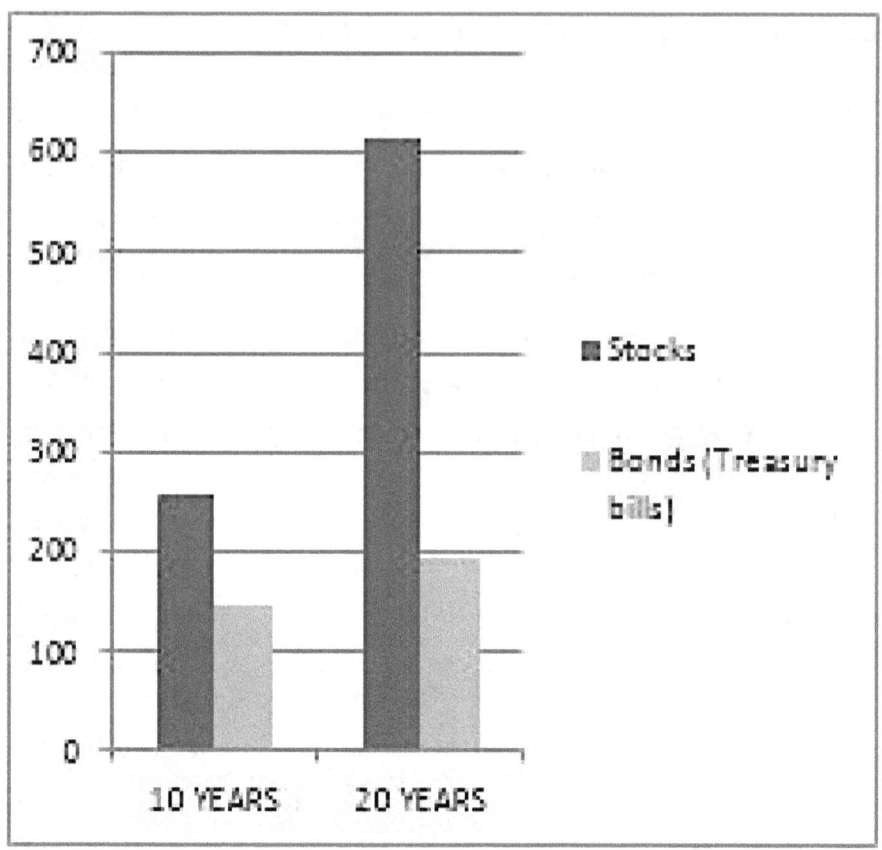

Return on investment for stocks versus short-term bonds

Investments are evaluated by the value for money that they generate for the investor above and beyond the inflation rate. Whatever the rate of inflation in a given year, it should be factored into the calculations when considering true returns. The stock market, therefore, presents all investors with value for their money in the form of greater rewards, a variety of investments that one can put their money into, like mutual funds, index funds, ETFs, international indexes, etc. Finally, the fees are considerably lower if you decide to go for discount brokers. More pricey stockbrokers also offer some investing advice, which is a surefire way to increase potential returns.

Dividends

A dividend is the share of a company's annual earnings that is shared out with the investors, with every share allocated a fixed payout depending on how much the company made that year. Dividends are viewed by most investors as free money because they add to your already appreciating initial investment whose value is dictated by the market forces in the stock market. For example, if you buy the stocks of company X for $50 and one year later, they have risen to $56, then that is an average rate of return of about 12%. However, if the company also issued a dividend payout of 3% on every share, then that is an extra 3% in returns that your investment just produced for you in that year. It is so great because a dividend is money you get on top of the nominal rate of return for your stock investment—free money, so to say.

The dividend is paid out in various forms, but the most prominent buyback and cash reward are the most common. In the cash reward option, the company credits every investor's account with a sum of money equivalent to the number of shares they hold with the company multiplied by the dividend payout rate. If the investor wants to reinvest this extra money back into the company, they can do so at their discretion. The buyback option is where a company offers investors with a dividend reinvestment plan to use their dividends to buy more shares at better terms.

The announcement date is the date on which a company discloses to the public that they intend to pay a certain amount of money to every shareholder. This payout is approved by the shareholders, so announcement dates usually come after the annual general meeting. The record date is the latest time an investor has to have bought the share for them to be eligible for the dividend. After a certain time, the ex-dividend date, shareholders are ineligible for dividends because they bought after the company had already settled on a certain rate based on the existing shareholder register. And of course, the payment date is the time at which the dividend payout is actually injected into the accounts of the shareholders. The definition of trading in the stock market encompasses all short-term stock investing, which is how we will compare it in this section. We shall assess the two forms of investment based on the four metrics—namely, time, profitability, risk, and complexity.

Pros and Cons

With short-term investing, the time it takes for your investment to bear fruit is much less. You could start a short-term investment portfolio and acquire positions in half a dozen companies with a maturity of two years or less. Rather than saving in the bank for a car or a family house, short-term investing can be a more profitable alternative. At the end of the two years, you could have made more money than you had benchmarked and buy a better house than you had planned or a pricier car. Or you could decide to reinvest the money for more gains.

With long-term investing, the focus is on the long run of up to twenty years. Some of the most popular long-term investments, like the 401(k) does not have an exit position any shorter than the twenty or so years it will take between getting employed and retiring. Others, like the Roth IRA, have a limitation of about five years. The time limitation makes a long-term investment rather lethargic, and people who burn out easily could give up halfway through the journey. This risk is less likely with short-term investing, which requires more active participation.

Even though it takes an awful lot of time, the amount of money you can make with long-term investment is very high. With the stock market growing an average of 11% every year, long-term investment of over twenty years will grow to three or four times its original size by the end based on the principles of compounding interest and dividend-reinvestment plans. The extra money that comes from dividends is especially attractive to investors as it is essentially free money that your investment makes for you. This is also why the 25× goal is possible; you invest enough of your current salary in dividend stocks until the dividend payout you receive is equivalent to your salary, then you can retire on the principal and still keep making money.

Short-term investments are significantly less profitable than long-term ones. But considering that they are most useful when saving up for a specific purpose, short-term investing is still more profitable than any other method of saving available out there. It is actually possible for a short-term investment to attain the gigantic profitability levels of long-term investments, but this would come with massive risks that could also spell doom for your whole investment objective.

As mentioned in the point above, short-term investments in the stock market are considered riskier. When invested in areas like treasury notes, money markets, certificates of deposit, and bond funds, the short-term investments are rather secure, if a little less profitable.

The risk in a long-term investment is determined fully by the investor themselves. After figuring out their risk tolerance, an investor then devices an investment strategy, then builds up their assets along specific risk lines. With an aggressive strategy, the risk is huge, but then so are the rewards. A balanced strategy promises average returns and minimized risk, while a conservative strategy accumulates low reward and minimal risk assets that generate a small profit.

The short-term investment landscape is significantly more complex than the long-term one. With so many things to consider and focus zoomed in on very tiny sections of the stock price chart, short-term investors have to contend with a constant barrage of concerns and things that need taking care of if they are to hope to make money off their investment.

Long-term investing is significantly less complicated. For those investors who use passive portfolio management strategies, the investment process is actually a matter of buying, waiting, and selling, with breaks in between to rebalance and reinvest accumulated dividends.

Chapter 9: The Most Common Mistakes in Stock Trading

Developing the right mindset is very important when you want to become a good investor. In the words of stock investment maestro Warren Buffet, *"You need to control your mind first before you can manage your money."* In psychology, we learn that our thinking style, the way we perceive the world around us, and our actions are very specific to our personality type. This simple philosophy explains every aspect of our lives— from the types of foods we love to our choice of dressing style, career, human interactions, etc. The investment domain is no different. The mindset with which you approach the task of investing is critical for success.

The danger of our limited perceptions of our minds is that we think and act in certain ways without being consciously aware of the reasons for this kind of behavior. Subliminal messaging from the environment, the vestiges of our childhood conditioning, education, morals, beliefs, and past experiences all affect the way we make decisions. And for those decisions you make in everyday life—which café to eat dinner, what color of clothes to buy, whether to order in or eat out or cook your own food and all other mundane decisions we make on a day-by-day basis—you can never be wrong. And when you are, at worst, you end up not enjoying your supper or colleagues mock your dress choice. In investing, the stakes are much higher.

All these emotions that inform the way we make choices and the specific choices that we make are essential in personal relations. In fact, a relationship devoid of emotions is likely to be stressful and draining. The inverse is also true for decisions we make concerning investments—emotions make us less effective money makers, at least in the financial market. Four basic emotions that you need to stay very wary of when venturing into the world of investment include greed, fear, hope, and ignorance. These emotions color our thinking in a very specific direction and cause us to miss very important signals that we are making a mistake.

Greed has the propensity to make people overcommit to promising investments. At the same time, it blinds us to the risks associated with a particular investment and makes us overcommit where we think we stand a chance of making good money. Greed alone is responsible for the formation of most investment bubbles. The concept of "the next big thing" plays on our greed and fear of missing out and causes us to pursue a course of action that an otherwise clear-minded person would avoid because they can spot the risks involved.

As mentioned above, fear also plays a part in our decision-making processes when participating in the financial markets. It comes in several forms, including the fear of missing out, the fear of failure, and surprisingly, the fear of success. It is because of fear that the stock markets react in a similar fashion when a traded company faces some negative publicity—batch selling. People also often sell their stocks at the first sign of trouble, forgetting the good things about a stock because their fears magnify the bad and cause it to look like an unattractive investment even when it is in fact very good. However, you can harness your fear as a force for good by forcing yourself to re-evaluate your choices to minimize risk whenever you feel that prick of fear, which is actually a good thing in the financial markets.

Hope is both a good and a bad thing. Every time we invest in an asset with the intention of holding on to it for a long time and make money afterward, this is an indication of hope. We hope that the investment we have made will reward us with a good return. Hope also helps us live through those daunting downturns in the stock market when our stocks plummet, and we fear that we will lose all our investments. But the best kind of hope is something that is rooted in solid research and confident information.

Without a proper understanding of the financial markets, the decisions we will make will be very bad. Ignorance causes us to rely on our own wits and idea of how things ought to be instead of how they are. Knowledge is power, and information is money, especially in the stock market. The informed person has a very big advantage over the one who operates blindly. So much so that the SEC has banned insider trading because the insiders are privy to so much information that it is not fair to the rest of the stock market. But with proper research skills, you can make decisions with the accuracy of an inside trader.

Here is how important mindset is. A study conducted by Harvard psychology professors put forward that if all the riches in the world were combined in one giant pool and distributed equally to every person on earth, the people who were previously wealthy would recoup their wealth within ten years. The poor would need just about the same time to end up back where they were before. The whole 1% debate draws great ire from "the rest," the people who feel that their boss's boss has taken from them and accumulated large amounts of money at their cost. Many politicians are building their political careers on the idea of increasing taxes on the wealthy and reducing inequalities. What they don't understand is that taking more from the rich won't deter them. Building wealth is a matter of having the right mindset, which obviously means that remaining poor boils down to having the wrong state of mind.

If this is the case, then why don't people simply change their state of mind and build wealth? Mostly, it is because a lot of people who languish in poverty do not understand that their own attitude is their worst enemy. So, they continue to blame the world, the economy, employers, parents, and pretty much anyone else but themselves for their misfortunes. The saddest part about this is that it blinds them to their role in their own mess and makes it quite impossible for them to extricate themselves from the vicious cycle. Another reason why we are not all rich is that the investor mindset is very elusive. It is also very hard to condition our minds to think right and enable us to make money through investing. However, if you are willing to learn and work for it, an investor's mindset is a surefire way to build yourself a small fortune.

To do this, you will have to develop your ability to make and stick to an action plan, harness the innate desire to succeed in every one of us, put together a "master mind alliance," learn to accept failure, and take action.

Creating an Action Plan

An action plan is like a destination when you are traveling somewhere. Without it, you may end up anywhere, and you would still not have reached your destination. In the process of creating an action plan, you will have to understand yourself and what you want. If you want to become a really good investor, you will have to do this for your life as well as your investment plan. A concrete plan transfers an idea in your mind into a compulsion that pushes you to act. Without an action plan, whatever you feel you should do remains an abstract idea that you will work on some time. The time could be any time in the future after some event has passed, or after you have attained a certain age.

But you will be surprised to learn that even after the condition you have set for yourself has been met, you will still be holding back. Psychologists have discovered the connection between current procrastination and future procrastination. If you put something off to do in the future, you are just as likely to put it off at the time when you set for yourself to do it because you have established a precedent. The way to develop an investor's mindset, therefore, is to formulate an action plan now and act on it the soonest possible time.

Harness the Desire to Succeed

The desire to succeed is inborn in every one of us, but a lifetime of conditioning has made us fall out of touch with this very primitive instinct. We all have that one thing that excites us. It could be that side project that you never tire of working on or the idea that excites you but you are too terrified to pursue. The thing about the desire to succeed is that it is easier to harness it when you are doing something you love. In the world of investment, the desire to succeed enables you to follow the path you set for yourself above toward creating wealth despite the hurdles that may come your way. To succeed in investing, you need to harness your desire to succeed in every activity you do as you follow the action plan you created for your life goals.

The Master Mind

The master mind is formed when a group of people with similar purposes (to succeed in life) form an alliance. It was first advanced by Napoleon Hill in the book *Think and Grow Rich*, a text that profiled the strategies followed by some of America's richest businesspeople. Your master mind group—whether it is your family, friends, business partner(s), or life coach—helps you to push yourself to achieve your goals. A mentor is one very important component of the master mind group, but if none is available, a similarly driven friend or a few of them can be very motivational too. When you associate with people who are as driven as you are to achieve success, you support each other and compete with each other at the same time—a very nice combination that can only send you shooting into the stratosphere.

Dealing with Losses

We have said it time and again, but risks abound in the stock market. You can expect to make losses at one point in your investment journey, but this does not matter one bit. What is important is the way you deal with these losses. Every investor has made a huge mistake in their investment journey that caused them to lose a lot of money, but by understanding that failure is inevitable, they were able to push ahead and make more money than they know what to do with. You probably don't want to engage in the stock market full-time. You may not have the time to learn the intricacies of investing, but learning to look at losses as imposters rather than the reality will embolden you to venture into the world of investing with confidence. And as you get better at investing, you will learn to deal with loss better and, with practice, even get very good at avoiding it for the most part.

Action!

Taking action, which must come right after formulating an action plan, is so important to deal with the rest of the issues discussed in this section. Because of the daunting nature of investing and the fears that we have about losing our hard-earned money, you might be tempted to leave your action plan as just a plan and neglect the action part of it. Procrastination has stolen many a dream from many people. At any one time, you can find at least five excuses to avoid jumping into the financial markets today. If it is not high interest rates, then it will be a recession. After that ends, the political field becomes too unpredictable, and you decide to wait for the next midterm or general election. Yes, knowing who our next head of state will be is important to my investment plan. On and on you go, making excuses and delaying the moment of action. And in the meantime, fantastic investment opportunities just keep on passing you by. It has been co-opted by one of the world's most iconic apparel brands, but the three-word sentence "Just do it" really does describe this process. Even if you have to dip your toes first with tentative speculation or a tiny investment, the time to start working toward your financial goals is now. And the investment sector is the way to reach there.

Controlling Emotions

Here is something that should interest you: we lose 13% of our IQ when faced with a financially stressful situation. At this point, we make terrible decisions that often carry serious consequences for us and our financial well-being. It is this kind of emotional thinking that causes people to buy during an upturn in the price of a stock, simply because the stock has risen in price and seems like such a good buying opportunity and sell when the price falls regardless of the factors behind the trend. An analytical mind would identify the downturn as the opportunity to buy up, taking advantage of lower prices to buy more shares per unit dollar. The same mind would know that, when it comes to liquidating, you sell at the earliest opportunity when the price goes past a certain point rather than waiting for the peak because you never know when a rise could turn into a sudden nosedive.

This small example illustrates two very interesting points. One, we make the exact opposite choices when we use our minds from the decision we make through analytical thinking. Two, the decisions we make using our emotions are almost assuredly always the wrong ones. Obviously, we need to set aside emotions and use our minds if we are to find success in investing. So how exactly do we do this?

Look at the Bigger Picture

The stock market is always responding to something. If you keep adjusting your investment strategies to correspond with every minute change, then you will spend your whole life as an investor scared stiff. The science backs this strategy. According to studies by behavioral experts at Brinker Capital, the chances of encountering a market in decline when you look at it daily are 46.7%. Taking the scrutiny back and assessing the market once a year brings the odds of encountering a declining market down to 27.6%. Those who look daily will see losses so much that they start anticipating them, terrifying themselves into making bad choices in the process, while those who occupy their minds with something else and look less frequently will remain in a state of serenity and optimism. The markets have encountered some very dramatic crashes in the past 35 years, but did you know that they closed 27 of 35 years with an improvement on the previous year? It would be hard to believe this after reading about the terrible losses suffered in the dot-com bubble burst, Black Monday, and the stock market crash of 2008, but stocks are generally great performers.

Don't Love Your Stocks

It is a sound piece of advice that enables you to stick it out with a stock you believe in when the rest of the world might be selling. However, emotional investors become very attached to their stocks. For a variety of reasons, including that a person loves the product the company sells or because the stock has been in their portfolio for over twenty years and used to give good dividends ten years ago, people often keep underperforming stocks in their portfolios long after they prove to be unsound.

Emotional attachment to a stock means that you neglect your most important responsibility in the investment process—to yourself and your money. By giving your emotions free rein to dictate your portfolio management, you jeopardize not only your current financial standing but also your entire future. The best form of investment is the one where all decisions follow a very logical line of reasoning rather than emotional sentiment.

Be Bold

To overcome the very influential emotions of fear and their power over our investment decisions, you will have to train yourself to be very bold. Herd mentality is very dangerous because it is formed by a cocktail of all four emotions discussed at the start of this chapter—fear, greed, hope, and ignorance. People are driven by the fear of missing out and the greed to invest in assets that they don't understand well. They trust in the rest of the market to be right and invest eagerly in the hope of a quick return. To overcome the herd mentality, you have to be bold enough not just to seek to stand out; you need to enjoy it. Standing out means that you are doing something different, which means that you will be in a position to take full advantage of whatever opportunities you find, away from the eyes of the public.

Ask Questions

Questions are the ingredients with which knowledge is built, and knowledge is the firm foundation for a profitable career in the financial markets. The most important question to ask about an investment before venturing forth is "How does this help me achieve my financial goals?" Along with this, figure out the worst- and best-case scenarios and try to imagine how your life would shape up in the worst-case scenario. Evaluate the answers to these questions in a very objective manner. Never hurry the decision-making process. It only makes you more nervous and increases the chances of you making the wrong one. Manage the pressure of the moment and carefully asses the options available to you, writing down the pros and the cons for a more insightful analysis. This way, when you finally get a move on, you will be certain as to what decision you ought to make.

Make Use of Your Master Mind

Even if you may get carried away, there are very few chances that your master mind partners will make the exact same thought patterns on an issue like you. Whenever you feel like you are getting carried away, consulting with the master mind can be the thing to give you clarity. The master mind relationship is supposed to be a nurturing one, so your master mind partners are likely to point out the emotions that influence your decision-making processes. If you are unsure, asking them point-blank will allow you to get an accurate, unrehearsed answer.

The Rule of Opposites

The rule of opposites is one that has made a fortune for numerous long-term investors in the stock market. The emotional nature of market reactions to signals, such as bad publicity and poor financial results released by an account, makes it very dangerous to follow the public. Warren Buffet stated this rule very succinctly, advising investors to practice massive caution when the rest of the market sees an opportunity for money-making and makes money on the fears of the market demonstrated by mass actions.

Transforming yourself from a beginner investor into a master in the snap of a finger is virtually impossible. Not even the best-written book on investment strategies can do that for you. The mastery of investment strategies comes from years of trial and error, with numerous losses made in between.

Conclusion

Even though a stock does not give the stockholder the right to take possession of a company's assets, it gives them the right to vote and take part in the decision-making process. There exist two types of stocks: the preferred stock and common stock. The common stock is the one that gives the holder the right to vote and have a part in the decision-making process during stockholder meetings, but they are also owners in the company, so their claim in the event of a dissolution or bankruptcy comes last. On the other hand, the preferred stock gives the holder the status of a lender, which means that they are paid first in the event of a dissolution or bankruptcy. Stocks are issued to help companies raise money through an intricate process known as the IPO. While the investment bank strategy of underwriting during initial public offerings is the more common of all issuance strategies, some companies choose to offer their shares directly to the public or leave the public to set their own prices through an auction. This initial price then forms the base price at which future trading will be conducted.

Bonds are issued by governments and corporate institutions that need to raise huge amounts of capital for massive expenditure. Investment is the most common motive behind bond issuance, but recurrent expenditures and debt restructuring is also a common motivation for a company or government issuing a bond. Unlike stocks, bonds mature at a set time, carry a specific interest or coupon yield, and are issued at fixed face value. The price fluctuations of bonds, while present, are very slight. They are usually caused by changing interest rates and demand close to maturity. There are two main types of bonds: *zero-coupon bonds*, which are issued at a discount to the yield, and *convertible bonds*, which allow holders to convert their bond capital into shareholding in a company.

The stock markets of the world started as a group of debt collectors organizing to renegotiate and exchange equity in ancient France. Over close to millennia, the stock market has spread to the rest of the world. Stock markets have also become more innovative, incorporating new technologies as they came up and growing through economic downturns, stock market crashes, and world wars. Currently, the world's stock markets are almost combined in one giant bourse, with mergers like the Euronext and NYSE in 2007 creating a transatlantic stock market. Other international stock markets include the NASDAQ OMX and Euronext itself, which combined the stock markets of Spain, Belgium, and the Netherlands. This linkage has not been without its fair share of complications. The stock market crashes of 1987 and 2008 affected large portions of the world bourses and shed off massive amounts of wealth from investors all around the world.

The End